Research Report No. 21

THE EXPANDED FIELD CONFIRMATION

by Horton Lee Sorkin, PhD

THE INSTITUTE OF INTERNAL AUDITORS, INC.
International Headquarters, 249 Maitland Avenue
Altamonte Springs, Florida 32701

ISBN 0-89413-066-8

Library of Congress Catalog Card Number 78-53651

IIA78039-Oct 78

FOREWORD

Past research indicates that audit evidence obtained with positive and negative confirmation formats is unreliable. Previous confirmation studies produced widely varying error detection rates that averaged 50.4% for positive formats and 35.7% for negative formats. These low rates present an issue of real concern to internal auditors.

The International Research Committee of The Institute of Internal Auditors undertook a new, comprehensive study to determine more precisely the error detection rates of both confirmation formats. In addition, the study attempted to determine if the rate could be improved by using a new format called *the expanded field*.

Significant improvement in the error rate was achieved using the expanded field confirmation format. This study shows how to improve the reliability of the confirmation instrument in order to obtain more reliable audit evidence.

The Institute of Internal Auditors, Inc., through its research committee, is constantly working to improve the internal auditor's tools and techniques. We hope this study will encourage auditors to experiment with the expanded field format and to reevaluate the use of positive and negative confirmation formats. Additional study relating to costs reduced by use of the expanded field format would be particularly useful.

Special gratitude goes to Horton L. Sorkin for his contribution. We also appreciate the cooperation of Northwest Bancorporation and its chief auditor, Roger N. Carolus, in making this study possible. In addition, we thank the IIA's Twin Cities Chapter, the firms of Peat, Marwick, Mitchell & Co. and Northwest Bancorporation for their financial support, and the members of the Twin Cities Chapter Research Committee for their help.

James R. Kelly, CIA, CPA
International President 1977-78
The Institute of Internal Auditors

ACKNOWLEDGMENTS

This study could not have been made without the encourage-ment, support, and ethical commitment to improved auditing of Northwest Bancorporation and its employees. More than anyone else, the good parts of the study belong to them. Regrettably, for reasons of privacy, I am unable to list the participating bank's employees. But I can and do thank Dick Aarnes, Joan Bank, Ralph Boehlke, Roger Carolus, Ginny Homuth, Eugene Jackels, Gerald Lee, Dorothy Meuwissen, and Charles Petry.

I appreciate the early encouragement this study received from Dr. Richard B. Lea of Peat, Marwick, Mitchell & Co., and the Twin Cities Chapter of The Institute of Internal Auditors.

I am indebted to the Peat, Marwick, Mitchell Foundation for its extensive funding and confidence in my ability as a researcher. Special thanks in this regard are given to Robert Elliott, J. A. Morgan, and Donald Welsch.

My thanks also to Professors Michael J. Barrett, Thomas J. Bouchard, Jr., Gordon B. Davis, Jack Gray, and Frank B. Martin, who served on my doctoral dissertation committee at the University of Minnesota. That dissertation was the basis for this monograph. Professors R. Glen Berryman, Norton M. Holschuh, Richard C. Miller, and C. David Vale, also of the University of Minnesota, provided further timely assistance and advice during the study. I am grateful to them.

There are four persons to whom I am particularly indebted. Kenneth Meuwissen of Northwest Bancorporation guided me throughout the study. Ken is my mentor, and, by his example, I feel I better know the meaning of professionalism.

Professor Jack Gray, my adviser at the University of Minnesota, was always available. Jack gave me his time and good advice, and helped keep things in perspective. I am fortunate to have had Jack as a teacher and adviser.

I am grateful to Professor Michael J. Barrett, whose early encouragement helped me define the scope of the study. I also am indebted to Professor Barrett for introducing me to Northwest Bancorporation personnel.

William E. Perry, IIA's director of professional practice, and members of The Institute provided a constructive review process that markedly improved the final product.

To my wife, Virginia, whose expertise in many fields proved invaluable, go special thanks.

Horton L. Sorkin, PhD
August 1978

ABOUT THE AUTHOR

Horton L. Sorkin, PhD, is on the faculty of the University of Kansas Graduate School of Business where he teaches auditing and cost and managerial accounting. Prior to receiving his PhD at the University of Minnesota, he attended the Wharton School of the University of Pennsylvania, University of Missouri, and Washington University.

Sorkin has over ten years' professional experience designing and implementing statistical quality control systems in industry and government. He has also been a consultant to industry, primarily in production planning and cost control systems. His more recent experience includes management in sales and wholesale distribution.

THE INSTITUTE OF INTERNAL AUDITORS
INTERNATIONAL RESEARCH COMMITTEE
1978-79

CONTENTS

EXHIBITS

TABLES

1 INTRODUCTION

A primary reason for auditing is to attest to the accuracy of an organization's records. One important means of determining this accuracy is to collect evidence through the use of confirmations — requests to external parties to compare the organization's records with their own for verification.

The negative and positive formats now used in these requests for verification (or confirmation) present problems for auditors if the external parties do not inform them of erroneous information on the requests. Auditors depend, in part, on the evidence they collect from confirmation responses to ascertain the accuracy of the business' booked account balances. If the evidence is unreliable, the auditor's credibility is compromised.

This report presents and examines findings of a study undertaken in the fall of 1976. The study's purpose was to document the unreliability of detecting account balance errors using positive and negative confirmation requests and to prove the greater reliability of a new confirmation technique: the *expanded field format*. The study showed the expanded field format is more efficient and significantly more effective in detecting erroneous account balances than either positive or negative confirmation formats. The effectiveness of the expanded field may allow the auditor to reduce sample sizes, and thus increase efficiency whenever third party verifications are used to determine accuracy of account balances.

The design of the study was simple. A bank's installment loan customers were mailed confirmation requests containing deliberate misstatements of their account balances. By measuring the rate at which customers informed the auditor of misstatements, inferences were made regarding the quality of evidence obtained from the use of various confirmation formats.

The expanded field format resulted from analyzing confirmation formats within a testing framework. Negative and positive formats are essentially true/false tests since recipients are asked to either confirm or take exception to an amount stated on the confirmation.

The negative format requests a reply only if the information is erroneous. The positive format requests a reply whether the information is correct or incorrect. The expanded field also requests a reply regardless of the accuracy of information, but the expanded field is a multiple choice test. The recipient must choose the correct amount from several stated amounts or take exception if all stated amounts are in error.

The study indicated that none of the three formats furnishes an auditor with completely reliable evidence of inaccurate bookkeeping. However, the expanded field format is significantly more reliable for collecting evidence than the positive or negative formats. Only 36% of those receiving positive requests informed the auditor of misstatements; 18% of the negative request recipients took exception. The expanded field format proved superior with 67% of the recipients taking exception to deliberately misstated amounts. The results are statistically significant because of the large number (1,920) of deliberately misstated requests mailed.

SUMMARY STATISTICS AND IMPLICATIONS

Statistics

Following is a tabulation of the account population used in the study and summary results:

Population: Installment loan accounts of a metropolitan bank
Outstanding balance: $3,565 average
No misstatement: 301 accounts analyzed
Comparative studies: 1,443 erroneous requests mailed for all five
    listed in Appendix A. This study is 12% larger than previous
    studies combined (1616 v. 1443)[1]

DETECTION RATES — PERCENT MAILED:

Large misstatements — Negatives - 16%
                      Positives - 41%
                      Expanded fields - 70%
Small misstatements — Negatives - 19%
                      Positives - 31%
                      Expanded fields - 62%

DETECTION RATES — PERCENT RESPONDENTS:

Large misstatements — Positives - 51%
                      Expanded fields - 95%
Small misstatements — Positives - 41%
                      Expanded fields - 83%

Response rates: No statistically significant difference between
    positives and expanded fields: overall study for above two
    formats 75.5%.

Implications

The detection rates associated with the expanded field format were superior to the rates associated with the positive format, and far superior to negative format detection rates. Assuming the results of this study persist across other account types and economic entities, the auditor's use of the expanded field format would result in a greater probability of detecting erroneously booked account balances for a fixed sample size than would use of positive or negative confirmations. Selecting a confirmation format would then depend primarily on a comparison of costs.

---

[1]A search of auditing literature revealed five studies of positives and/or negatives. They are: Roger R. Palmer, John Neter, and Gordon B. Davis, *A Research Study on the Effectiveness of Confirming Personal Checking Accounts* (Park Ridge, Ill.: The Association for Bank Audit, Control and Operation, 1967); Eugene H. Sauls, "An Experiment on Nonsampling Errors," in *Empirical Research in Accounting: Selected Studies* (Chicago: University of Chicago Press, 1971), pp. 157-171; Eugene H. Sauls, "Nonsampling Errors in Accounts Receivable Confirmation," *Accounting Review*, January 1972, pp. 109-115; Thomas D. Hubbard and Jerry B. Bullington, "Positive and Negative Confirmation Requests — A Test," *Journal of Accounting*, March 1972, pp. 48-56; Carl S. Warren, "Selection Among Alternative Confirmation Forms" (PhD dissertation, Michigan State University, 1973). Information found in the studies is included in Appendix A.

2 THE PROBLEM: UNRELIABLE EVIDENCE

The field study had two objectives: to measure more precisely the unreliability of positive and negative confirmations as evidence-collecting techniques and to determine whether confirmation technique reliability could be improved by using the expanded field format.

In this section we will define reliable evidence, establish a framework to characterize errors that create unreliable evidence, and analyze previous studies to establish that positive and negative confirmations can be unreliable.

ERRORS WITH CONFIRMATIONS

Need for Verifiable Evidence

The auditor collects and evaluates evidence to determine the accuracy of an organization's financial statements. Without evidence which can be verified, auditing loses its purpose. Verifiable data is data from which similar conclusions can be drawn when examined by two or more qualified people. Throughout this study it is assumed that audit evidence is always verifiable. Such data is essential to the auditor's function and the legal credibility of the auditor's opinions.

Need for Unbiased Evidence

Reliable evidence, in addition to being verifiable, must be unbiased.

To illustrate: Assume an adding machine always registers totals that are deficient by $10. Observers will agree on the totals the machine registers, even if they believe the totals are incorrect. The constant error of $10 is bias. The observers can remove the bias by repairing the machine or can compensate for it by adding $10 to each total. The auditor performs the observer's task in auditing by requiring removal or compensation for bias.

Thus, reliable evidence is both verifiable and unbiased. Verifiable evidence is reliable if no bias exists or existing bias is appropriately compensated for.

Types of Errors: A Framework

Biased evidence may be unreliable because bias results from errors. Confirmations will not yield reliable evidence if bias which cannot be compensated for is inherent in the confirmation process. Three errors which may occur in confirmations are sampling errors, nonresponse errors, and improper response errors.

Sampling Errors

Sampling errors occur if a portion of a population is tested, and an auditor characterizes the entire population from this portion. A complete census would have resulted in an appropriate characterization. Sampling can be used in auditing, and no attempt is made here to establish that sampling errors are a major problem in auditing or confirmations.

Nonsampling Errors

Nonsampling errors may be more critical to reliability than sampling errors. They occur in two forms — nonresponse and improper response — and may occur even if a census of the population, rather than a sample, is taken.

Nonresponse occurs when the recipient of a positive confirmation request fails to respond. The auditor can directly measure the nonresponse rates for positive confirmation requests because a reply is requested whether or not information on the form agrees with the recipient's records.

Nonresponses may lead to nonsampling errors with the use of positive confirmation requests. If all account holders are sent positive requests and only a portion are returned, it is not always justifiable to conclude that the number and type of discrepancies in the unreturned portion are proportionately the same as in the returned portion.

Improper Responses

Recipients of negative confirmation requests are asked to reply only if they disagree with the information on the request. Auditors generally consider a response improper if the information on the negative request is erroneous and no response is received. The auditor considers no reply as a verification from the recipient. For the negative format, therefore, the auditor assumes there is a zero nonresponse rate[2] and that the nonsampling errors are all improper responses.

Improper response occurs in three forms:
- *Task refusal* occurs when the recipient replies that he cannot or will not verify or take exception to the confirmation.

- *Type I Error* occurs when the recipient responds that the confirmation information is incorrect when, in fact, the information is correct.
- *Type II Error* occurs when the recipient responds that information is correct when it is incorrect.

These three types of improper responses create three different problems for the auditor

Task refusal leads to the type of error associated with nonresponses. Bias may result if the auditor generalizes results from the recipients performing the task with those who refused.

Auditors will recognize a Type I error (when the account is correct and the recipient takes exception) when the exception is reconciled with the organization's books. The extent and cost of Type I errors are thus subject to direct measurement.

Type II errors (when the recipient says that information is correct when it is incorrect) will go undetected unless discovered through alternative techniques. Type II errors are not normally detected in the confirmation process. However, their extent and cost may be subjectively estimated by the auditor. Table 1 summarizes Type I and Type II errors.

Table 1
Type I and Type II Errors

		True State of Account Balance	
		Correct	Incorrect
Confirmation Response	Reported Correct	No error in confirmation process	Type II (Not detected)
	Reported Incorrect	Type I (Detected)	No error in confirmation process

Empirically Determined Reliability

An analysis shows that the use of positive and negative confirmations does not provide the auditor with reliable evidence. For this analysis, reliable evidence from confirmations is defined as the absence of Type II errors. The analysis data is derived from five empirical studies of confirmation reliability, summarized in Appendix A.

A 1966 study by Roger R. Palmer, John Neter, and Gordon B. Davis simulated erroneous bookkeeping by deliberately misstating external parties' account numbers on confirmation requests. Responses were analyzed to determine the rate at which misstatements were detected. Four subsequent studies duplicated this experimental method, although the account balances were only misstated.

All these studies showed that the use of the positive confirmation format does not provide the auditor with completely reliable evidence. The net rate of Type II errors, when used as one measure of positive confirmation reliability, is determined by dividing the number of recipients who do not inform the auditor of a discrepant request by the total number of recipients who respond. The net rate of Type II errors averaged 49.6% across the studies, varying from 17% to 74%. Only about half the recipients informed the auditor of the erroneously stated information. These results cannot be used as a basis for bias compensation due to the variability of the error rates.

Use of the negative format also may not provide reliable evidence. All nonrespondents are assumed to agree with the information on the confirmation. In the case of the negative format, the net Type II error rate is calculated by dividing the number of recipients not informing the auditor of a discrepancy by the number of negative requests mailed. The net Type II error rate for negatives averaged 64.3% across the studies, varying from 56% to 83%. Only about one-third of the recipients informed the auditor of erroneously stated information. Compensation for bias in Type II errors again is not feasible due to variability in the error rate.

In one sense, the Type II error measures the recipient's tendency to agree with or "say yes" to the information contained in the confirmation request. The auditor, concerned with the accuracy of an organization's books, is limited in the use of confirmations when recipients fail to report the existence and extent of errors. Based on the five studies reviewed, bias appears to be inherent in the confirmation technique. It also appears that bias cannot be precisely compensated for because of wide variations in Type II error rates. Thus, positive and negative confirmations are not reliable evidence-collecting techniques.

---

[2]Alvin A. Arens and James K. Loebbecke, *Auditing: An Integrated Approach* (Englewood Cliffs, NJ: Prentice-Hall, 1976), p. 330.

3 A SOLUTION: THE EXPANDED FIELD

The auditor uses the confirmation technique to gather evidence to evaluate the accuracy of an organization's books. Empirical studies show that confirmations furnish the auditor with unreliable evidence when the organization's books are inaccurate. Unreliable evidence also results from Type II errors, the recipient's confirmation of erroneous information.

This chapter examines task requirements for positive, negative, and blank confirmation requests. It is assumed that Type II errors for positives and negatives result partially from respondents' inclination to say yes to the information on the request. The possibility of preventing this behavior by forcing the respondent to confirm one amount from many will be discussed. Including multiple amounts on a confirmation request expands the respondent's decision field in comparison to the single amount on the positive or negative request and provides more reliable evidence by reducing Type II error rates.

Task Requirements for Present Formats

The recipients of positive or negative confirmation requests are asked to compare information on the requests with that in their own records. If the information in their records disagrees with that on the requests, they are directed to write a detailed explanation in the space provided for comments on the requests, and then sign, date, and mail the forms to the auditor. To encourage returns, stamped envelopes addressed to the auditor are usually furnished.

The recipients of negative confirmation requests need not respond if their records agree with information on the requests. Task requirements for the negative requests are thus specified. Exhibit 1 is an example of negative format instructions.

Recipients of positive confirmation requests are directed to respond whether their records agree or disagree with information shown in the request. If records agree, they sign, date, and mail the confirmations to the auditor. If records disagree, they detail the discrepancy in the space provided and sign, date, and mail the confirmations to the auditor. Exhibit 2 is an example of positive format instructions.

Exhibit 1
Negative Instructions

---

    1. COMPARE THE INFORMATION SHOWN BELOW WITH YOUR RECORDS FOR THE DATE INDICATED.

    2. IF THERE ARE ANY DIFFERENCES, PLEASE GIVE FULL DETAILS IN THE COMMENTS SPACE BELOW.

    3. PLEASE SIGN, DATE, AND RETURN THIS FORM DIRECTLY TO THE AUDITOR   ***ONLY IF THERE IS AN ERROR***

        ****THIS IS NOT A REQUEST FOR PAYMENT****

COMMENTS:

CURRENT BALANCE AS OF NOV. 5, 1976 $3,862.28

Exhibit 2
Positive Instructions

---

    1. COMPARE THE INFORMATION SHOWN BELOW WITH YOUR RECORDS FOR THE DATE INDICATED.

    2. IF THERE ARE ANY DIFFERENCES, PLEASE GIVE FULL DETAILS IN THE COMMENTS SPACE BELOW.

    3. PLEASE SIGN, DATE, AND RETURN THIS FORM DIRECTLY TO THE AUDITOR. A SELF-ADDRESSED ENVELOPE HAS BEEN PROVIDED FOR YOUR CONVENIENCE.

        ****THIS IS NOT A REQUEST FOR PAYMENT****

COMMENTS:

CURRENT BALANCE AS OF NOV. 5, 1976 $4,110.10

Reason for Errors

The task requirements for either the positive or negative formats are straightforward. If the task is done correctly, erroneous information on the confirmation request should be detected. The preceding chapter's examination of earlier studies revealed that recipients of requests with erroneous information did not always detect errors. Assuming the recipients' records are correct, their agreement to erroneous confirmation requests can be explained in one of two ways.

First, the recipients may compare the confirmation with their records, detect a discrepancy, and decline to inform the auditor. Possible reasons for this include:

- The errors are in the recipients' favor, and they believe it advantageous not to have the audited organization's books corrected.

- The recipients perceive the error as small and not worth the effort required to inform the auditor.

- The recipients conclude their records are incorrect, and the discrepancies are the result of their own poor record keeping or performance of the requested task.

Second, recipients of erroneous requests may fail to report a discrepancy because no comparison of records was made. If erroneous negative requests are received and no comparison made, the recipients simply do not return the request to the auditor. In this case, nonresponse is considered verification, resulting in a Type II error.

If erroneous positive requests are received and no comparison made, the recipients may do one of two things. They may not return the request, which results in nonresponse, or they may return the request without comparing their own records. The latter results in verification and, thus, a Type II error.

Verification of a positive request tells the auditor that the recipient agrees with the information on the request. Recipients of a positive request who hesitate to question the information on the request and simply date, sign, and mail the request are characterized as exhibiting "say yes" behavior. The task for say yes respondents is thus unambiguous.

Criteria for a Solution

Any change in confirmation format that reduces the respondent's ability and eagerness to say yes should increase the confirmation technique's reliability in detecting discrepancies. Two lines of reasoning suggest that this will happen. First, a respondent may perform the comparison, detect errors, and note the discrepancy on the confirmation, increasing the net detection rate. Second, the recipient may decline to respond, increasing the net detection rate by definition.[3]

A Solution With Total Ambiguity

The positive request is not open to interpretation if recipients want to say yes because there is only one amount they are asked to confirm. The say yes respondents' actions indicate to the auditor that the amount on the request is correct. One way to prevent say yes behavior is to make the confirmation totally unclear concerning the account balance in the audited organization's books. Use of the blank format requires recipients to tell the auditor what is in their personal records. While this format has appeal, it appears to be an expensive alternative for two reasons.

First, the Type I errors might increase. The auditor must spend additional effort to determine whether the recipients are correct when they provide information disagreeing with correct organization books.

Second, the auditor must spend further effort by using alternate means to determine the accuracy of an account if a response is not received.

Research indicates the number of nonrespondents increases when the blank format is used.[4]

A Solution With Limited Ambiguity

Say yes behavior can also be discouraged by introducing limited uncertainty about the customer's account balance on the audited organization's books. Exhibit 3 represents a confirmation format with limited uncertainty. With this format, the current practice of including correct information from the organization's books is maintained by recording it as one of the amounts on the request. Say yes recipients of positive confirmation requests are limited in possible reactions when faced with such a request.

One possible reaction is refusal to respond, in which case the Type II errors for those recipients are reduced to zero if errors exist on the organization's books. This results because a Type II error occurs only if recipients confirm accounts that are incorrect. If recipients do not respond, they do not confirm.

Another possible reaction is correct performance of the task by a recipient whose personal records are correct. In this case, the Type II error is again reduced to zero because existing discrepancies would be detected and reported to the auditor. The net detection rate then increases since the rate is a function of the number of detections.

Recipients may incorrectly perform the task and question information on the request due to poor task ability or inaccurate personal records. If the organization's books are correct, Type I errors, which are exceptions to correct information, would increase.

If the books are incorrect, Type II errors may be reduced when the auditor uses alternative procedures to determine if the exception is proper. The reply or the books may provide enough evidence for the auditor to conclude that an error exists.

The recipient may circle a guessed-at amount or one considered favorable. If the books are correct, this increases Type I errors by definition. If the amount reflecting an organization's incorrect books is randomly assigned as an amount on a request similar to that in Exhibit 3, there is a chance that a Type II error will occur one-third of the time. By the very nature of the expanded field, the chance of randomly choosing the correct amount from the three choices is one in three. The effectiveness of the auditor's alternative procedures determines whether the auditor can ascertain if the books are incorrect when a respondent circles an amount other than the one the auditor believes is correct. Thus, for this final case, the reduction of Type II errors is not determinant.

For all behavioral patterns of say yes recipients faced with the expanded field format, Type II errors are either reduced or produced at the same rate expected with the use of positive requests.

The Expanded Field

"Expanded field" is a term derived from the field of alternatives from which the recipient may choose. The expanded field confirmation format is shown in Exhibit 3.

Exhibit 3
Expanded Field Instructions

1. COMPARE THE INFORMATION SHOWN BELOW WITH YOUR RECORDS FOR THE DATE INDICATED.

2. IF NONE OF THE AMOUNTS AGREE WITH YOUR RECORDS, PLEASE INDICATE THE BALANCE SHOWN BY YOUR RECORDS.

3. PLEASE SIGN, DATE, AND RETURN THIS FORM DIRECTLY TO THE AUDITOR. A SELF-ADDRESSED ENVELOPE HAS BEEN PROVIDED FOR YOUR CONVENIENCE.

****THIS IS NOT A REQUEST FOR PAYMENT****

COMMENTS:

CURRENT BALANCE AS OF NOV. 5, 1976

*** CIRCLE THE CORRECT AMOUNT ***

$3,763.82 $3,961.92 $4,160.02

In positive or negative formats there is only one signal (amount) in the recipient's decision field. The requested response is true/false or two-part.

The blank format is a large expansion of the number of signals in the recipient's decision field, a reasonable characterization if one considers that a great number of possible monetary amounts could be reflected correctly or incorrectly on the organization's books. The response asked for in a blank format request is multiple choice because the recipient is asked to furnish an answer from a large number of feasible choices.

Compared to the positive and negative formats, the expanded field is a limited expansion of the number of signals (three) in the recipient's decision field. Recipients are asked to select from multiple choices: agreeing with any or none of the three amounts. This expansion of the number of signals in a confirmation, compared to the single signal of the positive or negative formats, creates the expanded field.

Simulation of Behavior

The behavior of recipients of positive or expanded fields is simulated by diagram to allow further consideration of the differences in behavior.

Because this study mainly concerns detection of errors in an organization's books, it is assumed that all requests contain erroneous information.

Exhibit 4 simulates behavior of recipients of positive requests containing erroneous information. Explanations of terminology used in the exhibit are:

Receive 2nd request — After an appropriate time the auditor again contacts those who did not respond to the initial requests.

Compare to records — The recipients compare their own records with the information on the requests.

Say yes — The recipients agree with information on the requests without comparing it to their own records or comparing it and not having sufficient faith in their records to inform the auditor of a discrepancy.

Contact issuer — The recipients contact the organization to compare the requests to the organization's records rather than to their own records.

Refuse task — The recipients consciously refuse to reply to the request.

Utility function — Recipients refuse to respond to the request in an unbiased manner. For instance, they may only take exception to a confirmation when a discrepancy is unfavorable to them.

Task ability — The recipients have task ability if they have a

Exhibit 4
Simulation of Behavior: Positive Confirmation

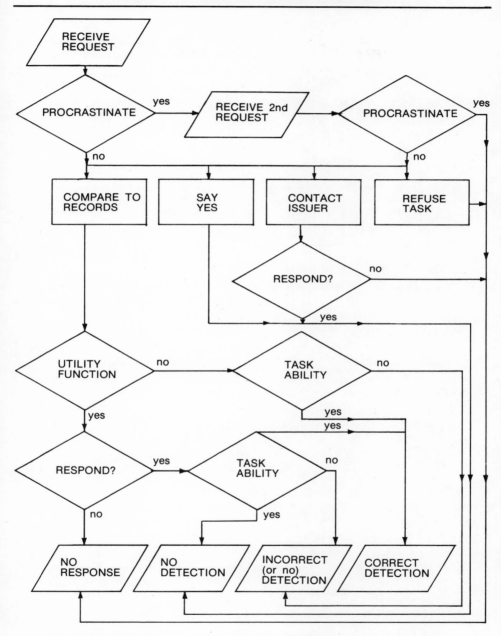

INCORRECT DETECTION = f (task difficulty, incomplete or incorrect knowledge, purposeful behavior)

Reception and response frequencies can be compromised by the quality of the communication channels (for example, incorrect addresses or unreliable mail).

Exhibit 5
Simulation of Behavior: Expanded Field Confirmation

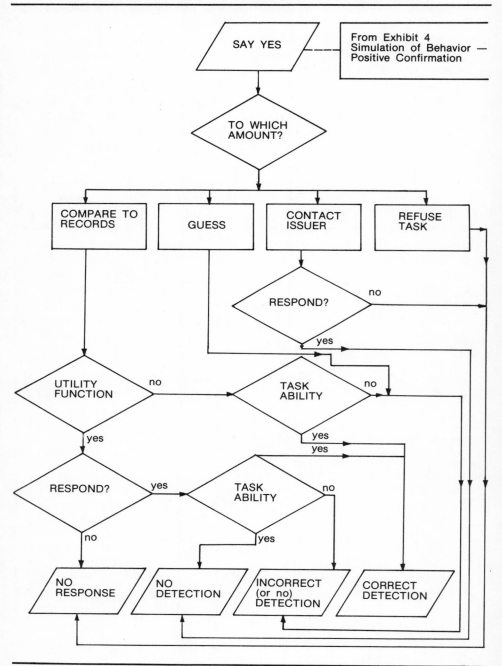

16

correct set of records and are able to correctly follow instructions on the request.

Exhibit 5 simulates behavior of the recipients of erroneous expanded field requests who would normally say yes to a positive request. Because of the expanded number of signals, they can no longer simply agree with information on the request, but must either choose one amount or take an exception if they wish to respond. Say yes respondents to positive requests tend to cooperate and follow the instruction to respond. This tendency might motivate recipients to follow all instructions when an expanded field is received. If this occurs, use of the expanded field should reduce Type II errors. It is also safe to assume that curiosity could motivate the say yes recipient to perform the comparison task correctly on receiving an expanded field request.

Analysis Limitations

This analysis of recipient behavior is limited. The question of recipient motivation and perception of confirmations has not been completely analyzed. Why anyone responds correctly to a confirmation, or refuses to respond, or performs the task erroneously is open to conjecture. The desirability of the expanded field depends, in part, on the validity of assuming that say yes behavior exists and can be converted into proper task performance behavior through use of the expanded field format.

---

[3]Net detection rate is a function of detections divided by responses. If the number of say yes respondents becomes nonrespondents, mathematically the detection rate must increase if four conditions hold. The four conditions are that errors exist in the organization's books, that some recipients' records are correct, that some recipients have performed the task associated without error, and that respondents advised the auditor of errors.

[4]For empirical data on blanks see Carl S. Warren, "Selection Among Alternative Confirmation Forms" (PhD dissertation, Michigan State University, 1973), pp. 33-5, 43-5, 90, 107.

4 DESCRIPTION OF THE FIELD STUDY

The field study undertaken in fall 1976 attempted to determine the reliability of error detection in three confirmation formats. Of the 2,280 confirmation requests mailed, 1,917 were judged suitable for analysis. Of the 1,917 suitable requests, 1,616 contained deliberately misstated account balances. An average large error of $110.97 was included with 805 discrepant requests, and the remaining 811 were misstated by an average small error of $4.80. The remaining 301 requests contained correct information. The confirmation recipients were installment loan customers of a large metropolitan bank.

Because the study's major goal was to determine the possibility of improving error detection reliability of currently used confirmation formats, it attempted to follow currently used procedures. The study followed a time sequence of a normal confirmation effort and used typical confirmation text material on the requests. Few restrictions were imposed on the study, and a complete cross section of normal installment loans was included with the exception of a small group of commercial leasing accounts.

The following section presents:
- an outline of appropriate experimental methodology
- a description of the participating institution and the sequence of the study's events
- a descriptive analysis of the accounts used in the study

METHODOLOGY

Common auditing practice is to send confirmation requests to external parties that accurately reflect information on the audited organization's books. The auditor uses confirmations in anticipation that recipients, after comparing confirmation information with their personal records, will inform the auditor of any difference. If this response contains sufficient information for the auditor to conclude that a discrepancy exists and the organization's books are incorrect, then the auditor has detected an error in the books. A confirmation effort's reliability decreases when the information received is insufficient to detect an existing error in the books. This nondetection was earlier defined as a Type II error.

The field study was undertaken to determine whether Type II error rates are reduced or, conversely, if confirmation reliability is increased when the auditor uses the expanded field instead of the positive or negative formats.

A Type II error can occur only when an organization's books are incorrect. However, to test reliability, erroneous bookkeeping may be simulated by mailing confirmations with misstated information. The recipient believes that the information received is directly from the books. Even if the books are correct, they appear incorrect to the recipient because of the deliberate misstatement on the confirmation request.

Appropriate methodology for measuring Type II error rates of various confirmation formats requires that confirmations containing deliberately misstated information be mailed and responses analyzed.[5] This is the methodology used in the field study.

STUDY PARTICIPANTS

The commercial institution participating in this study was a Midwestern metropolitan bank with assets totaling approximately $250,000,000. The bank had received the highest possible rating in an August 1976 audit. The auditors, therefore, believed the account balances used in the study to be correct. This is obviously a highly desirable situation because a study adding errors to an error-filled population would be difficult to justify and control.

Installment loan accounts were chosen for the study for six principal reasons:

- The available account population was large enough to accommodate the experiment.
- The volatility of account balances in other types of accounts could result in more erroneous confirmation responses.
- Confirmations are required for these accounts; thus, the study would follow current auditing practice.
- Loan customers' payment books would provide the study population with accurate records of current account status.
- The bank's management believed few customer relations problems would occur as a result of the study's using these particular accounts.
- The account type, being similar to populations in two previous studies of confirmation reliability, would allow comparison.[6]

During September 1976, an analysis was made of the number of accounts available for the study. The Installment Loan Department was found to have 11,655 active accounts, and all but 2,776 of them were eliminated. The types of accounts eliminated and the rationale for their elimination are summarized in Table 2.

Accounts were deleted from the study if the customer had not been issued payment books, or if books were possibly erroneous, because inaccurate personal record systems would make the comparison task difficult. Legally inactive loans, such as student loans, newer simple interest loans with interest calculated on the daily outstanding balance, and recently paid-off zero-balance loans were all eliminated for not meeting the study's requirements that recipients have an active loan and be able to perform the task easily. Leasing units were also eliminated at the bank management's request.

Table 2
Accounts Eliminated From Study

Account Type	Elimination Rationale
Ready reserve	No payment books
Executive credit	No payment books
Student loans	Inactive payment process
Leasing units	Customer relations problems
Post 6-30-76 loans	Written as simple interest
Zero-balance loans	Possible negative balances

These eliminations resulted in the study population of 2,776 in mid-September. However, loans were being paid off and closed out and new simple-interest loans were excluded from the study. Therefore, an estimated maximum 2,400 accounts were available for the study on November 10, 1976.

EXPERIMENTAL DESIGN

Criteria
Three criteria were used to design the experiment:
- The accounts were to be randomized to eliminate bias in the assignment of formats.
- All request recipients were to have payment books, enabling them to perform the required comparison.
- Each recipient was to be contacted regarding the status of only one loan account balance, preventing interaction among formats if a customer received more than one request.

Independent Variables

Magnitude of Errors
Magnitude of deliberate discrepancies was set at three levels: none, small and large. When no discrepancy existed, the amount on the confirmation request was the same as the account balance recorded in the bank's books. The purpose of including no-

discrepancy confirmation requests in the study was to establish response and Type I error base rates for positive and expanded field requests.

The small error discrepancy was defined as 2% of the account balance up to a maximum of $4.87. These errors simulated discrepancies due to handling charges for late payments or small errors in the bank's data processing. The large error discrepancy was defined as 6% of the account balance up to a maximum of $154.63. The large errors simulated discrepancies in handling loan payments at the bank.

During the September payment cycle, $4.87 was the average miscellaneous charge and $154.63 was the average payment received by the bank. Two percent and 6% were arbitrarily determined during a meeting with bank personnel. Percentage constraints were required to prevent small loan balances from becoming negative when discrepancies were introduced.

Direction of Errors

Two directions of errors — high and low — were possible when discrepancies were introduced into the account balances and were included in the study. High error was defined as an inflation of the actual account balance and low error as a deflation of the actual account balance.

A high error represents an error not in the customer's favor since the customer appears to owe the bank more than the account balance. Conversely, a low error represents an error in the customer's favor since the customer apparently owes less than the correct loan balance.

Confirmation Formats

The bank's internal auditors use forms similar to those shown in Exhibits 6 and 7. These forms are addressed for use in window envelopes and require no folding, for minimal handling. Information is printed on both sides of the form and includes a variety of data concerning the account. A self-addressed, stamped return envelope is sent with the request to encourage responses.

The positive and negative forms used in this study are shown in Exhibits 8 and 9. Among departures from current practice were:

- including only the name, address, account number and balance as information specific to the account
- using a letter- or standard-size form
- printing only on one side of the form
- triple-folding the form to fit window envelopes
- using no preprinting or varied typefaces on the form

Exhibit 10 shows the expanded field form used in the study. Basically the same as the positive form used, it differs in its second instruction and contains three amounts rather than one.

Exhibit 6
Currently Used Positive Format

SIDE 1

NORTHERN NATIONAL BANK

INSTALLMENT BANKING   472-8031

7th STREET

ANYTOWN, USA 55480

AUDIT CONFIRMATION

SEE REVERSE SIDE FOR DETAILS

TYPE OF ACCOUNT INSTALLMENT LOAN	AUDIT DATE 12-28-73

LOAN NUMBER	0001000029	REGULAR PAYMENT AMOUNT	53.07
ORIGINAL LOAN BALANCE	1,910.00	NO. OF PAYMENTS REMAINING	15
CURRENT LOAN BALANCE	796.13	NEXT PAYMENT DUE DATE	02-16-74
LATE CHARGES DUE	.00		

NOTE - YOU MAY HAVE ADDITIONAL LOANS CARRIED UNDER OTHER LOAN NUMBERS

SAM JONES

RT 5

LONE PINE, USA

PLEASE REPLY DIRECTLY TO:

SAM AUDITOR

ROOM 816

ANYTOWN BANK BUILDING

ANYTOWN, USA 55480

    THIS IS NOT A REQUEST FOR PAYMENT

SIDE 2

THIS CONFIRMATION IS A REGULAR AUDIT PROCEDURE TO PERIODICALLY CONFIRM BANK RECORDS. PLEASE CONFIRM THE CORRECTNESS OF THE INFORMATION SHOWN ON THE FRONT SIDE OF THIS FORM AS FOLLOWS:

1. COMPARE THE INFORMATION SHOWN WITH YOUR RECORDS FOR THE DATE INDICATED

2. IF THERE ARE ANY DIFFERENCES, PLEASE GIVE FULL DETAILS IN THE COMMENT SPACE BELOW.

3. SIGN, DATE, AND RETURN THIS FORM DIRECTLY TO THE AUDITOR. A SELF-ADDRESSED ENVELOPE HAS BEEN PROVIDED FOR YOUR CONVENIENCE.

THE INFORMATION AS OF THE DATE INDICATED IS CORRECT: ☐ YES   ☐ NO

COMMENTS:

Authorized Signature	Date	Address (if other than shown)

Exhibit 7
Currently Used Negative Format

SIDE 1

NORTHERN NATIONAL BANK
INSTALLMENT BANKING   472-8031
7th STREET
ANYTOWN, USA 55480

AUDIT CONFIRMATION
SEE REVERSE SIDE FOR DETAILS

TYPE OF ACCOUNT INSTALLMENT LOAN	AUDIT DATE 12-28-73

LOAN NUMBER	0001000029	REGULAR PAYMENT AMOUNT	53.07
ORIGINAL LOAN BALANCE	1,910.00	NO. OF PAYMENTS REMAINING	15
CURRENT LOAN BALANCE	796.13	NEXT PAYMENT DUE DATE	02-16-74
LATE CHARGES DUE	.00		

NOTE - YOU MAY HAVE ADDITIONAL LOANS CARRIED UNDER OTHER LOAN NUMBERS

SAM JONES
RT 5
LONE PINE, USA

PLEASE REPLY DIRECTLY TO:
SAM AUDITOR
ROOM 816
ANYTOWN BANK BUILDING
ANYTOWN, USA 55480

THIS IS NOT A REQUEST FOR PAYMENT

SIDE 2

THIS CONFIRMATION IS A REGULAR AUDIT PROCEDURE TO PERIODICALLY CONFIRM BANK RECORDS. PLEASE COMPARE THE INFORMATION SHOWN ON THE FRONT OF THIS FORM WITH YOUR RECORDS FOR THE DATE INDICATED.

IF THERE ARE ANY DIFFERENCES, PLEASE GIVE FULL DETAILS IN THE COMMENTS SPACE BELOW, SIGN AND RETURN THIS FORM TO THE ADDRESS SHOWN ON THE FRONT SIDE.

IT IS NOT NECESSARY TO RETURN THIS FORM IF THE INFORMATION IS CORRECT.

COMMENTS:

Authorized Signature	Date	Address (if other than shown)

Exhibit 8
Positive Format Used in Study

XYZ Bank
111 Main Street
Metro, U.S.A.

** AUDIT CONFIRMATION **

DEAR CUSTOMER:

TO ASSIST US IN OUR CONTINUING AUDIT PROGRAM FOR YOUR PROTECTION, PLEASE CONFIRM YOUR INSTALLMENT LOAN ACCOUNT.

1. COMPARE THE INFORMATION SHOWN BELOW WITH YOUR RECORDS FOR THE DATE INDICATED.

2. IF THERE ARE ANY DIFFERENCES, PLEASE GIVE FULL DETAILS IN THE COMMENTS SPACE BELOW.

3. PLEASE SIGN, DATE, AND RETURN THIS FORM DIRECTLY TO THE AUDITOR. A SELF-ADDRESSED ENVELOPE HAS BEEN PROVIDED FOR YOUR CONVENIENCE.

**** THIS IS NOT A REQUEST FOR PAYMENT ****

_____

COMMENTS:

_____

AUTHORIZED SIGNATURE   DATE   ADDRESS(if other than shown)

THANK YOU FOR YOUR COOPERATION.
THE INTERNAL AUDITORS OF XYZ BANK.

ACCOUNT NUMBER 00123456789

CURRENT BALANCE AS OF NOV. 5, 1976 $4,110.10

Charles Customer
2222 Home Avenue
Anywhere, U.S.A.

Exhibit 9
Negative Format Used in Study

XYZ Bank
111 Main Street
Metro, U.S.A.

** AUDIT CONFIRMATION **

DEAR CUSTOMER:

TO ASSIST US IN OUR CONTINUING AUDIT PROGRAM FOR YOUR PROTECTION, PLEASE CONFIRM YOUR INSTALLMENT LOAN ACCOUNT.

1. COMPARE THE INFORMATION SHOWN BELOW WITH YOUR RECORDS FOR THE DATE INDICATED.

2. IF THERE ARE ANY DIFFERENCES, PLEASE GIVE FULL DETAILS IN THE COMMENTS SPACE BELOW.

3. PLEASE SIGN, DATE, AND RETURN THIS FORM DIRECTLY TO THE AUDITOR   *** ONLY IF THERE IS AN ERROR ***

**** THIS IS NOT A REQUEST FOR PAYMENT ****

COMMENTS:

AUTHORIZED SIGNATURE   DATE   ADDRESS (if other than shown)

THANK YOU FOR YOUR COOPERATION.
THE INTERNAL AUDITORS OF XYZ BANK.

ACCOUNT NUMBER   00123456789

CURRENT BALANCE AS OF NOV. 5, 1976 $3,862.28

Charles Customer
2222 Home Avenue
Anywhere, U.S.A.

Exhibit 10
Expanded Field Format Used in Study

XYZ Bank
111 Main Street
Metro, U.S.A.

** AUDIT CONFIRMATION **

DEAR CUSTOMER:

TO ASSIST US IN OUR CONTINUING AUDIT PROGRAM FOR YOUR PROTECTION, PLEASE CONFIRM YOUR INSTALLMENT LOAN ACCOUNT.

1. COMPARE THE INFORMATION SHOWN BELOW WITH YOUR RECORDS FOR THE DATE INDICATED.

2. IF NONE OF THE AMOUNTS AGREE WITH YOUR RECORDS, PLEASE INDICATE THE BALANCE SHOWN BY YOUR RECORDS.

3. PLEASE SIGN, DATE, AND RETURN THIS FORM DIRECTLY TO THE AUDITOR. A SELF-ADDRESSED ENVELOPE HAS BEEN PROVIDED FOR YOUR CONVENIENCE.

**** THIS IS NOT A REQUEST FOR PAYMENT ****

COMMENTS:

AUTHORIZED SIGNATURE   DATE   ADDRESS (if other than shown)

THANK YOU FOR YOUR COOPERATION.
THE INTERNAL AUDITORS OF XYZ BANK.

ACCOUNT NUMBER   00123456789

CURRENT BALANCE AS OF NOV. 5, 1976

*** CIRCLE THE CORRECT AMOUNT ***

$3,763.82 $3,961.92 $4,160.02

Charles Customer
2222 Home Avenue
Anywhere, U.S.A.

Two variations were used with the expanded field; a 5% spread or a 10% spread, with each larger amount being 5% or 10% greater than the lower adjacent amount (see Table 3). Spreads were included to determine whether additional research using this treatment might be worthwhile.

No attempt was made to vary the number of amounts or signals for the expanded field. The use of three amounts was recommended by several educators, practitioners, and businessmen. Also, three amounts simplified the projected statistical analysis and the computer programming necessary to generate the expanded field requests.

Sample Size in Experimental Cells

Given the number of accounts available for study and the formats and their variations listed, the actual partitioning of the accounts into formats was clear-cut. Twenty format variations were possible, giving 120 accounts per variation. However, to leave a safety margin, if fewer than the projected 2,400 accounts were available when the actual study was run, the number of variations, or number of accounts per variation, would be decreased. The correctly stated negatives were deleted from this study because Type I error levels associated with negative format were not of major concern.

Table 3 shows the experimental design used for the study. The design varied the direction and amount of deliberate misstatement for all three formats. As noted earlier, the percentage of discrepancy between the amounts in the expanded field format was also varied. Presently used positive and negative formats were included to analyze the desirability of the new format without having to refer to previous studies for data.

Cell Control

Before the accounts were partitioned into formats, the total account population was randomized using a computer algorithm furnished by James K. Loebbecke of Touche Ross & Co. The randomization was performed by calling the experimental population by account number, then using the algorithm for programming efficiency. No attempt was made to directly control the dollar amounts in each experimental cell for three reasons:

- The bank could not make the necessary adjustments in its own computer files to accomplish this control.
- The bank's data base could not be taken off premises to accomplish this control due to privacy constraints.
- The effectiveness of randomizing the total population reduced the necessity for dollar amount cell control.

Table 3
Experimental Design[a]

Confirmation Type	Error[b]	% Spread[c]	Cell Sample Size[d]
Positive	None	--	120
Positive	Small high	--	120
Positive	Large high	--	120
Positive	Small low	--	120
Positive	Large low	--	120
Negative	Small high	--	120
Negative	Large high	--	120
Negative	Small low	--	120
Negative	Large low	--	120
Expanded field	None	5%	120
Expanded field	None	10%	120
Expanded field	Small high	5%	120
Expanded field	Large high	5%	120
Expanded field	Small low	5%	120
Expanded field	Large low	5%	120
Expanded field	Small high	10%	120
Expanded field	Large high	10%	120
Expanded field	Small low	10%	120
Expanded field	Large low	10%	120
		Total	2280

[a] On all expanded field confirmation requests, the appropriate accounts are to be partitioned uniformly among the three decision points.

[b] Small error is the smaller of 2% of the correct balance or $4.87. Large error is the smaller of 6% of the correct balance or $154.63.

Percent spread is the distance between the amounts in the expanded decision field. For example, if the correct amount balance was $100.00, the error was "large high," and the percent spread was 10%, the amounts in the expanded field confirmation would be either ($100 × 6% = $106.00):

$ 84.80	$ 95.40	$106.00
or: $ 95.40	$106.00	$116.60
or: $106.00	$116.60	$127.20

[d] Sample size is predicated upon a response rate of approximately 75%. Some uneven shrinkage of cell sizes will occur since duplicate accounts will not be eliminated until the analysis stage of the study. Overall shrinkage is estimated to be 7%.

Printing of Confirmations

Exhibit 11 shows the computer logic used to generate the confirmation requests. This logic was part of implementing the experimental design shown in Table 3. The computer was programmed to print confirmation requests. The positive and expanded fields were printed in duplicate so that second requests would be available to send to recipients not responding to initial requests.

Letter of Explanation

Exhibit 12 shows the letter of explanation sent to all recipients of confirmation requests. The letter was sent immediately to reduce any anxiety about receiving a confirmation request containing discrepancies and to inform the customer of the reason for the different size form in the case of positives or negatives, or the unique form in the case of expanded fields.

The letter was mailed within a day after receipt of the customer's phoned or mailed reply. At the conclusion of the study, explanatory letters were mailed to all remaining customers. The possibility that receipt of an explanatory letter might cause experimental interaction with other customers who had not yet replied was considered negligible. This risk was taken because all connected with the study felt it important to alleviate adverse customer reaction.

Telephone Monitoring

A telephone monitoring diary system was installed in the bank to handle adverse customer reaction and to maintain experimental control. Since information regarding the status of an installment loan could be sourced in only one bank area, switchboard operators were instructed to direct all incoming calls regarding active installment loans to this area. Three or more members of management were always available to speak with callers.

Customers who called concerning a confirmation were asked for their loan account number, informed of the study and its purpose, and asked for their reaction. The customer was also promised a letter of explanation. Information relevant to each telephone inquiry was manually recorded in the diary to insure the letter was sent, and inquiry information was kept for later analyses.

Experimental considerations required that recipients who called the bank be eliminated from the study's response and detection rate analysis. This was necessary for two reasons. First, recipients requesting the bank's balance of their account could not be assumed to have compared the information on the confirmation request with their own records. Confirmations received from customers who made a telephone inquiry were considered to reflect

Exhibit 11
Computer Logic

Logic for Confirmation Experiment Utilizing Strata and Mark IV Software

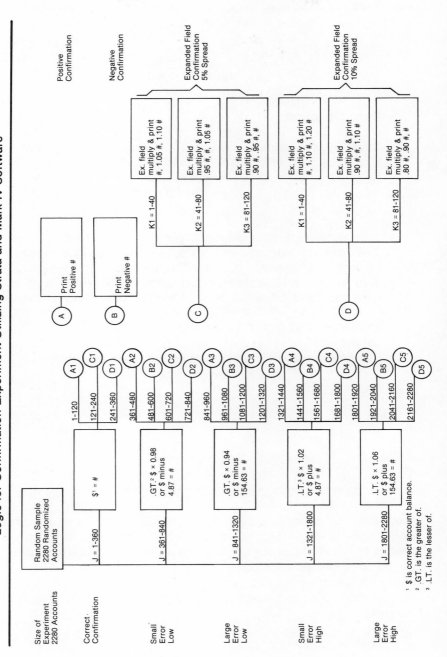

Exhibit 12
Letter of Explanation

XYZ Bank
111 Main Street
Metro, U.S.A.

Dear Customer:

Recently, our auditor sent you a confirmation request
This was part of a research project being carried on
by our bank. Some of the confirmation requests had
data which did not agree with the actual balances of
the account.

The purpose of this research project was twofold.
The primary purpose was to determine that our record
of your account was correct. The secondary purpose
was to help us decide whether asking customers to
confirm their accounts is an effective procedure.

I want to thank you personally for your help. I
believe that this type of research can improve both
our service to and protection of you, our customer.

Sincerely,

President

---

bank records rather than the requested comparison of customer's
and bank records. Second, telephoning customers were told the
nature of the study, and it was assumed that reluctance to inform the
auditors of errors decreased.

Controls were also in place to monitor replies of customers who
visited the bank or mailed letters to the bank rather than to the
auditor.

Sequence of Events

Table 4 summarizes the sequence of events from the generation
of the requests to the conclusion of the study.

Table 4
Sequence of Events (1976)

Date	Study Day	Event
November 9		Requests printed with 11/8 balances
November 10	0	2,280 requests mailed
November 11	1	First telephone calls received
November 12	2	First mail responses received
November 25	15	Second requests sent to positive and expanded field nonresponders
November 26	16	Cutoff date for analyzing negatives
December 10	30	Cutoff date for analyzing positives and expanded fields

The sixteenth day of the study marked the final day that negative responses could be used for analysis, since letters of explanation were then sent to all nonresponding recipients of negative confirmations. It was assumed that any responses to negatives would thereafter be compromised by the explanation. Explanatory letters were sent to nonrespondents of positive and expanded field requests on the thirtieth day of the study, excluding any further responses from analysis and marking the end of the study. This time sequence parallels the normal time sequence of a confirmation effort by a bank's internal auditors.

Final Size of the Study

When the study was designed in September 1976, 2,400 accounts were estimated to be available. In actuality, 2,404 accounts were available. Approximately 7% of the accounts were estimated to represent duplicate loans held by one person, family, or company as determined from a sample of the 11,655 accounts in the Installment Loan Department.

Included in the 2,280 requests mailed were 281 confirmation requests sent to customers who received more than one request or format variation. This represented a 12.3% reduction of the study population to 1,999 accounts available for analysis. The estimation error occurred because duplicate accounts were found to be heavily concentrated in the types of accounts used in the study. These accounts were manually eliminated because relevant data was not accessible from the computer files.

An additional 52 accounts were eliminated because confirmation recipients telephoned. The final cut eliminated 30 accounts because of mail delivery delays, bringing the final size of the study used for analysis to 1,917 accounts. They are partitioned in Table 5.

Table 5
Final Size of Study

Error Treatment	None	Small Low	Large Low	Small High	Large High
Expanded Field Format					
Number of Accounts	203	203	190	199	201
Positive Format					
Number of Accounts	98	100	100	101	107
Negative Format					
Number of Accounts	N.A.	111	106	97	101

Total Number of Accounts: 1,917

Randomization Checks

Since the study assumed that format variations were randomly assigned to the population, an analysis was performed after the study to confirm the randomization. The analysis was conducted in three ways. First, loan balances were divided into eight dollar-amount levels and analyzed by means of a chi-square test against the 14 treatment categories shown in Table 5. Then, the types of installment loans were separated into the bank's 24 collateral categories for similar analysis. Finally, the dollar-amount of error variance was categorized into 10 dollar-amount levels and analyzed against treatments for small and large error randomization. The analysis determined that the study did have randomized treatments.

Description of the Study Population

The following population description, while not extensive, provides sufficient information for comparing the 1,917 accounts used in the analysis with other account populations.

The mean balance of the accounts used in the study was $3,565. The 95% confidence interval for the mean is from $3,323 to $3,808. Table 6 summarizes the distribution of the dollar balances of the 1,917 accounts used in analysis.

The two major loan-type categories in the study were *direct* and *indirect*. The 1,450 direct loans were the result of direct application by loanholders to the bank. The 467 indirect loans resulted from intermediary institutions' commercial transactions with customers being financed by bank installment loans. All loan customers had been furnished a loan contract and made payments directly to the bank for either type of loan.

Table 6
Distribution of Account Balances

Category	Percent
$200.00 or less	2.2
$200.01 to $500.00	7.5
$500.01 to $1,000.00	12.9
$1,000.01 to $2,000.00	22.6
$2,000.01 to $5,000.00	36.6
$5,000.01 to $10,000.00	12.1
$10,000.01 to $20,000.00	5.0
$20,000.01 and more	1.1
Total	100.0

The reasons for issuing the 1,917 loans are shown in Table 7 in descending order of percentage and represent a combination of the bank's 24 collateral categories.

Table 7
Reason for Loan Request

Reason	Percent
Used automobile	34.8
New automobile	20.1
Unsecured personal	8.5
Commercial equipment	6.9
Home improvement	6.6
Household goods	4.9
Secured personal	4.8
Mobile home	4.5
Recreational equipment	4.2
Work-out loans	1.7
Real estate	1.2
Unsecured commercial	1.0
Employment fees	0.5
Farm equipment	0.3
Total	100.0

The error variations were distributed among the accounts according to Table 8. The average deliberate discrepancy for the small error variation was $4.80. For the large error variation, the average deliberate discrepancy was $110.98.

Two descriptive statistics were derived from the address labels of the 1,917 loan customers. It was found that 10.4% of the loans were addressed to commercial institutions, 22.7% to couples, 52.3% to males and 14.6% to females. In addition, 9.9% were found to have mailing addresses outside the state.

Table 8
Distribution of Dollar Errors

Amount of Error	Small Error (811 Accounts)	Percent
$1.00 or less		0.1
$1.01 to $2.50		1.1
$2.51 to $4.86		2.3
$4.87		96.5
Total		100.0
Amount of Error	Large Error (805 Accounts)	Percent
$4.87 or less		0.3
$4.88 to $30.00		9.2
$30.01 to $60.00		13.2
$60.01 to $90.00		10.3
$90.01 to $120.00		11.4
$120.01 to $154.62		9.8
$154.63		45.8
Total		100.0

[5]Roger R. Palmer, John Neter, and Gordon B. Davis, *A Research Study on the Effectiveness of Confirming Personal Checking Accounts* (Park Ridge, IL: National Association for Bank Auditors and Comptrollers, 1967), p. 5.
[6]See Appendix A for the results of loan account studies conducted by Eugene H. Sauls and Carl S. Warren.

5 STUDY RESULTS

The results of this study indicate that the expanded field format is significantly more reliable than either the positive or negative formats. The Type II error rates, whether gross or net, associated with the expanded field were a small fraction of the rates experienced with the use of the other two formats.

The detection ability of the expanded field was also superior to either the negative or positive fields, regardless of the amount or direction of error variations. Even without the use of second requests, the expanded field was significantly more reliable than either of the other two formats.

The major limitation of the expanded field was a Type I error rate twice as great as that experienced with correctly stated positives.

This section presents data matrices derived from the study and analyses of the results. The statistical methodologies used for the analyses are the chi-square test and hierarchical log-linear modeling for statistical significance.[7]

Spread in the Expanded Field

One experimental treatment in this study was the inclusion of 5% and 10% spreads between the amounts in the expanded field format. No prior hypothesis was offered concerning the effect of varying the spread, and no opinions were presented by anyone surveyed prior to the actual study. Thus, null hypotheses were tested that no response or detection differences existed between the two spread variations.

Statistically, the hypothesis that no differences in response types result from varying the amount of spread could not be rejected. Since the spread variations created no apparent differences, the data concerning the expanded field will not be partitioned along this dimension in the analyses to be discussed later.

The Data Matrix

Table 9 is the frequency data matrix for all formats, error variations, and responses. Table 10 is the percentage data matrix derived from the frequencies in Table 9 and measures developed in Appendix B. Table 10 shows that gross and net Type II error rates are lower for expanded fields than for either positives or negatives.

ANALYSIS

Response Rates: Expanded Field, Positive

Response rates are important to the auditor. When recipients of a positive or expanded field do not respond, the auditor must use alternate procedures to ascertain the accuracy of nonrespondent account balances. If a significant difference exists in the response rates of the two formats, other things being equal, then the format resulting in a lower response rate would be more expensive for the auditor to use.

Prior to the study, opinions were mixed concerning the effect of the expanded field on response rates when compared to the positive's response rate. Three major reasons were given for expecting a declining response rate using the expanded field. First, some expanded field recipients would not respond because the requested task would appear more difficult. Second, a lower level would respond because say yes recipients would still decline to perform the comparison and simply discard the request. Third, some recipients might view the expanded field as insulting and not respond.

Two major reasons were given for a possible increased response rate. First, a recipient's curiosity might be aroused by the increased ambiguity in the expanded field. Such a recipient might be more inclined to perform the task and respond. Second, there might be response from recipients who believed the auditor was more concerned about a response, as indicated by the increased complexity of the new expanded field format.

Chi-square tests indicated there was no significant difference in response rates between positives and expanded fields. The major departure was the high 83.8% response rate associated with the positive format for the large high error variation. Although an 83.8% rate is not unexpected, it might be statistically useful to determine whether the higher response rate for this variation would occur if this study were repeated.

Gross Detection Rates for Three Formats

Nonrespondent negative format recipients are generally assumed to have verified the confirmation request. Thus, detection rates for negatives are calculated by dividing the number of respondents

Table 9
Study's Overall Data Matrix (Frequencies)

FORMAT	EXPANDED FIELD					POSITIVE					NEGATIVE			
ERROR TREATMENT	None	Small Low	Large Low	Small High	Large High	None	Small Low	Large Low	Small High	Large High	Small Low	Large Low	Small High	Large High
Total mailed	203	203	190	199	201	98	100	100	101	107	111	106	97	101
Did not reply	49	49	53	52	50	21	26	23	22	17	91	91	76	82
Refused task	2	5	4	2	1	1	1	1	0	2	0	0	1	0
Verified request	132	23	9	25	4	71	50	47	40	34	91	91	76	82
Detected error	----	123	114	113	136	----	23	29	39	54	20	15	20	19
Type I error*	10	----	----	----	----	5	----	----	----	----	----	----	----	----
Amount right,* wrong circle	10	----	----	----	----	----	----	----	----	----	----	----	----	----
Amount wrong, wrong circle	----	3	10	7	10	----	----	----	----	----	----	----	----	----

* Respondents who took exception to all three amounts *and* respondents who circled a "wrong" amount on correctly stated expanded field requests are classified under Type I error percentages in Tables 10 and 12.

Table 10
Study's Overall Data Matrix (Percentages)

FORMAT	EXPANDED FIELD					POSITIVE					NEGATIVE			
ERROR TREATMENT	None	Small Low	Large Low	Small High	Large High	None	Small Low	Large Low	Small High	Large High	Small Low	Large Low	Small High	Large High
Response rate	75.6	75.9	71.5	73.6	75.0	78.4	73.7	76.8	77.2	83.8	100.0	100.0	100.0	100.0
Gross detection	----	63.6	66.7	60.9	73.0	----	23.2	29.3	38.6	51.4	18.0	14.2	20.8	18.8
Net detection	----	84.6	93.2	82.8	97.3	----	31.5	38.2	49.4	61.4	18.0	14.2	20.8	18.8
Gross Type II	----	11.6	4.8	12.7	2.0	----	50.5	47.5	39.6	32.4	82.0	85.8	79.2	81.2
Net Type II	----	15.4	6.8	17.2	2.7	----	68.5	61.8	50.6	38.6	82.0	85.8	79.2	81.2
Gross Type I	10.0	----	----	----	----	5.2	----	----	----	----	----	----	----	----
Net Type I	13.2	----	----	----	----	6.6	----	----	----	----	----	----	----	----
Task refusal	1.0	2.5	2.1	1.0	0.5	1.0	1.0	1.0	0.0	1.9	0.0	0.0	1.0	0.0

furnishing sufficient information for the auditor to conclude the request was misstated, by the number of misstated requests mailed. This method of calculating detection rates, called the Gross Detection Rate in Appendix B, was used in conjunction with log-linear modeling to determine the following statistically significant conclusions:

Format: For all types of errors included in the study, the expanded field is the superior error detection instrument. The positive format, while not as good as the expanded field, is better than the negative format.

Size of error: Large errors are detected more frequently than small errors with both the expanded and positive fields. Error size did not affect negative detection rates.

Direction of error: The detection rate for positives increases when misstatement is high or is not in the recipient's favor. Direction of the error did not seem to affect the detection rates of the expanded fields or negatives.

Any explanations for these results would be conjecture since no attempt was made to determine the reasons for recipients' behavior. The increased detection reliability associated with the expanded field probably resulted from substituting say yes behavior with proper confirmation task performance by the recipients. The positive format appears superior to the negative mainly due to inclusion of second request data.

Negative rates probably are not sensitive to the size and direction of the misstatements because negative format recipients tend to disregard requests entirely. In other words, the negative instruction to respond only if an exception is noted causes most recipients to discard the notice without checking their records.

Increased detection rates for the expanded field and positive formats when the error was large might indicate that the error must reach an appreciable amount before respondents will take the trouble to document an exception. The tendency of positive format respondents to more readily inform the auditor of errors not in their favor indicates that third parties are biased toward themselves. The complexity of the correct balance being mingled with several erroneous amounts in the misstated expanded fields apparently negated the biased response tendencies experienced with positives.

Net Detection Rates for Two Formats

The net detection rate was analyzed because a response was requested for expanded and positive fields whether or not the recipient detected an error. As a result, auditors can use these two formats and have additional information concerning the recipient's tendency to respond. Net detection rates for these two formats are described in Appendix B. Basically, the rate is the number of respondents who furnish sufficient information for the auditor to conclude that the request was misstated, divided by the number of responses to the misstated requests. Log-linear modeling was used to arrive at the following statistically significant conclusions:

Format: For all types of errors, the expanded field is a superior error detection instrument when compared to the positive.

Size of error: With either format, an approximate 10% increase in net detection rates occurs when the error is large rather than small.

Direction of error: Net detection rates for the positive format increased when the error was not in the recipient's favor, regardless of the error size. This effect was not significantly present with the use of the expanded field.

Interpreting results using net rather than gross detection rates did not change the previous interpretation: the expanded field is superior in detecting errors; the error must reach an appreciable sum before recipients will respond; and respondents are biased toward themselves.

Resistance to the Expanded Field

One obvious indication of resistance to a confirmation request occurs when the recipient refuses to confirm it or take exception, and notifies the auditor of this behavior. Prior to the field study, some persons believed that recipients would react negatively to the new format and behave in this manner.

Of the expanded field recipients, 1.4% replied with task refusal. The task refusal rate was 1.0% with positive recipients. This rate difference is not statistically significant. Thus, one may conclude that resistance to the expanded field format is no greater than to the positive.

A lower response rate for expanded fields compared to positives might indicate resistance to the new format. Even though the overall response rate for positives was 3.7% higher, the difference again was not statistically significant. Results indicate that the expanded field does not create more resistance than the positive format.

Looking at respondents' cooperation with, rather than resistance to, use of the expanded field, a different conclusion might be drawn. The significantly superior error detection rates experienced with the expanded field indicate more correct and thorough recipient task performance than with either the positive or negative format. Overt recipient resistance is no greater with the expanded field, and overt cooperation is greater.

Type I Errors — a Problem

A Type I error, or a respondent's exception to a correctly stated confirmation request, requires extra auditor effort to determine that the audited organization is correct and the external party is wrong. Substantial costs may be added by checking Type I errors. The costs may be alleviated if the auditor first undertakes a confirmation effort and then includes the accounts associated with Type I errors in a subsequent evaluation of internal controls.

For both the correctly stated expanded field and positive formats, 5% of the recipients incorrectly took exception and gave a documented response. However, an additional 5% of the expanded field recipients circled one of the two incorrect amounts. This caused the Type I error rate to be twice as great with the expanded field as with the positive. Thus, the expanded field is significantly inferior to the positive when measured by Type I error rates.

The auditor may use a smaller sample with the expanded field due to its markedly superior error-detection reliability. If this is done, costs associated with increased Type I errors can be offset by the savings in using a smaller sample size. These costs can be further offset by including Type I error accounts in a subsequent evaluation of internal controls.

Effect of Second Requests

The Palmer-Neter-Davis study, referred to in Chapter 2, concluded that using second requests with the positive format increased its reliability as compared to the negative. In this study, using the cutoff date of November 26 (16 days after study began), all three formats were analyzed to determine their reliability without using second request data. Tables 11 and 12 summarize the frequency and percentage results of this analysis.

The overall gross detection rate was 23.2% for positives and 17.8% for negatives. Positive reliability is only slightly better than negative reliability if second requests are not used, and gross detection rate is the reliability criterion. There is essentially no difference in reliability if the positive format's reliability in detecting large high errors is ignored.

However, the average net Type II error rate was 46.0% for the positive and 82.2% for the negative. Using this measure, the positive is more reliable than the negative. Since net rates are accessible to the auditor in evaluating evidence and characterizing populations, the positive format is preferable even if second requests are not used.

The overall gross detection rate was 44.7% for expanded fields and 23.2% for positives. It may be concluded that the expanded field is significantly more reliable than the positive, even without use of second requests.

The average response rate for the expanded field format was 6.3% higher than for the positive format. The average net Type II error rate was 35.6% lower for the expanded field than for the positive. Thus, the expanded field was significantly more reliable than the positive. In effect, the expanded field is also significantly more reliable than the negative, even if expanded field second requests are excluded from analysis.

---

[7]See Horton L. Sorkin, "An Empirical Study of Three Confirmation Techniques: Desirability of Expanding the Respondent's Decision Field" (PhD dissertation, University of Minnesota, 1977), pp. 123-148, for a description of the statistical methodology and analyses used in this study.

Table 11

Data Matrix After Eliminating
Data From Second Requests (Frequencies)

FORMAT	EXPANDED FIELD					POSITIVE					NEGATIVE			
ERROR TREATMENT	None	Small Low	Large Low	Small High	Large High	None	Small Low	Large Low	Small High	Large High	Small Low	Large Low	Small High	Large High
Total mailed	203	203	190	199	201	98	100	100	101	107	111	106	97	101
Did not reply	96	98	100	99	97	50	63	53	61	55	91	91	76	82
Refused task	2	3	1	2	0	0	1	1	0	0	0	0	1	0
Verified request	97	18	3	18	2	43	19	30	16	15	91	91	76	82
Detected error	----	82	82	76	94	----	17	16	24	37	20	15	20	19
Type I error	5	----	----	----	----	5	----	----	----	----	----	----	----	----
Amount right, wrong circle	3	----	----	----	----	----	----	----	----	----	----	----	----	----
Amount wrong, wrong circle	----	2	4	4	8	----	----	----	----	----	----	----	----	----

Table 12
Study's Data Matrix After Eliminating Data From Second Requests (Percentages)

FORMAT	EXPANDED FIELD					POSITIVE					NEGATIVE			
ERROR TREATMENT	None	Small Low	Large Low	Small High	Large High	None	Small Low	Large Low	Small High	Large High	Small Low	Large Low	Small High	Large High
Response rate	52.2	51.0	47.1	49.7	51.7	49.0	36.4	46.5	39.6	48.6	100.0	100.0	100.0	100.0
Gross detection	----	42.0	45.5	40.6	50.7	----	17.2	16.2	23.7	43.8	18.0	14.2	20.8	18.8
Net detection	----	82.4	96.6	81.6	98.1	----	47.2	34.8	60.0	71.2	18.0	14.2	20.8	18.8
Gross Type II	----	9.0	1.6	9.1	1.0	----	19.2	30.3	15.8	14.0	82.0	85.8	79.2	81.2
Net Type II	----	17.6	3.4	18.4	1.9	----	52.8	65.2	40.0	28.8	82.0	85.8	79.2	81.2
Gross Type I	4.0	----	----	----	----	5.1	----	----	----	----	----	----	----	----
Net Type I	7.6	----	----	----	----	10.4	----	----	----	----	----	----	----	----
Task refusal	1.9	2.9	1.1	2.0	0.0	0.0	2.7	2.1	0.0	0.0	0.0	0.0	1.0	0.0

6 CONCLUSIONS

The purpose of this study was to document the unreliability of positive and negative formats in detecting errors and to prove that the expanded field provides the auditor with a more reliable error detection technique. The research did not attempt to justify the use of confirmation requests or to recommend the use of confirmations. This and previous studies clearly indicate that positive and negative formats do not provide the auditor with completely reliable evidence about the accuracy of account balances. The positive is superior to the negative primarily because second requests are used.

The study does indicate that the expanded field, though not completely reliable, is superior to the positive except for a higher Type I error rate. The expanded field is superior to negatives even if second request data is excluded.

RECOMMENDATIONS

Based on results of this study and the assumption that the same results would occur with other account populations; and assuming the continued required use of confirmations by the auditor, the following recommendations are offered:

1. Because expanded fields are more reliable, use of positives is discouraged. Even though positives appear less costly because of a lower Type I error rate, this saving is offset by the increased sample sizes needed to compensate for the positives' lesser error detection reliability. Sample size considerations are discussed in Appendix C.

2. Because of the cost savings associated with the use of negatives, no recommendation is offered. The savings result from not using the second requests and alternate procedures that are used with positives and, presumably, expanded fields. If second requests are eliminated, and the auditor either characterizes nonrespondents by a small sample or makes no attempt to characterize, then the expanded field may prove definitely superior to negatives on a cost/benefit basis.

3. The auditor should determine whether the confirmation effort will occur before, during, or after the evaluation of internal controls. The cost structure of confirmations and the entire audit effort may be different depending on sequencing rules used by the auditor.

4. As this and previous studies prove, it cannot be assumed that nonrespondent recipients of negatives have correctly verified the requests. The credibility of evidence derived through use of negatives is questionable, although it appears neither logical nor desirable for the auditor to attempt to characterize negative nonrespondents.

5. Using appropriate sampling techniques, the auditor might select a sample of nonrespondents to positive and expanded field requests to characterize the entire population of nonrespondents. This should reduce costs.

APPENDIX A

Recapitulation of Empirical Confirmation Studies

The following notes identify the empirical confirmation studies charted on the following pages.

1. Gordon B. Davis, John Neter, and Roger R. Palmer, "An Experimental Study of Audit Confirmation," *Journal of Accounting*, June 1967, pp. 36-44. The study used personal demand deposit accounts of The First National Bank of St. Paul, Minnesota.

2. Eugene H. Sauls, "Nonsampling Errors in Accounts Receivable Confirmation," *Accounting Review*, January 1972, pp. 109-115. The study used personal and automobile loan accounts of the Continental Illinois National Bank and Trust Co. of Chicago, Illinois.

3. Eugene H. Sauls, "An Experiment on Nonsampling Errors," *Empirical Research in Accounting: Selected Studies*, (Chicago: University of Chicago Press, 1971), pp. 157-171. The study used time deposit accounts of the Michigan State University Employees Credit Union of East Lansing, Michigan.

4. Thomas D. Hubbard and Jerry B. Bullington, "Positive and Negative Confirmation Requests — A Test," *Journal of Accounting*, March 1972, pp. 48-56. The study used accounts receivable of the Consolidated Oil Company of Lynchburg, Virginia.

5. Carl S. Warren, "Selection Among Alternative Confirmation Forms," (PhD dissertation, Michigan State University, 1973). Studies five and six used share and loan accounts of the Michigan State University Employees Credit Union of East Lansing, Michigan.

Appendix A

Recapitulation of Empirical Confirmation Studies
(Blank Confirmations Excluded)

STUDY (All positives are for first and second requests, except Sauls-Bank.)

#	Study Excluded	Study Averages	STUDY	1 — 1966 Davis, Neter, Palmer	2 — 1967 Sauls Bank	3 — 1968 Sauls Credit Union	4 — 1971 Hubbard, Bullington	5 — 1972 Warren Loan Accounts	(5,6)	6 — 1972 Warren Share Accounts
1			Total population	847		478	825	700		700
2	2	705	Sampling population	847		456	825	326		326
3		324	Actual sample used			109	204			
4	2	185.6	Total positives sent	350	130	109	102	182		185
5	2	151.6	Total positives received	317	130	102	88	125		126
6	2	81.7	% response (5/4) positive	90.6	*	93.6	86.3	68.7		68.1
7		68.3	Correct positives sent	150	100	50	34	36		40
8		56.3	Total correct positives received	134	72	48	27	27		30
9		82.4	% response (8/7)	89.3	72	96	79	75		75
10		0	Type I positives received	0	0	0	0	0		0
11		0	% type I (10/8) positives	0	0	0	0	0		0
12	2	123.6	Incorrect positives sent	200	30	59	68	146		145
13	2	98.4	Total incorrect positives received	183	13	54	61	98		96
14	2	79.6	% response (13/12)	91.5	NA	92	90	67		66
15	2	49.6	Incorrect positives identified	118	13	45	33	27		25
16	2	50.4	% normal (net) detection (15/13) positive	64	?100	83	54	28		26
17	2	40.1	% gross detection (15/12) positive	59	NA	76	49	18		18
18	2	49.6	% type II normal (13-15/13) positive	36	NA	17	46	72		74
19	2	59.9	% type II gross (12-15/12) positive	41	NA	24	51	82		82
20	1,2,5,6	31.5	High incorrect positives sent	NA	30	29	34	NA		NA
21	1,2,5,6	28	High total incorrect positives received	NA	13	26	30	NA		NA
22	1,2,5,6	89	% response high (21/20)	NA	NA	90	88	NA		NA
23	1,2,5,6	18.5	High incorrect positives identified	NA	13	20	17	NA		NA
24	1,2,5,6	66	% normal detection (23/21) high positive	NA	?100	77	57	NA		NA
25	1,2,5,6	59	% gross detection (23/20) high positive	NA	NA	69	50	NA		NA
26	1,2,5,6	34	% type II normal (21-23/21) high positive	NA	NA	23	43	NA		NA
27	1,2,5,6	41	% type II gross (20-23/20) high positive	NA	NA	31	50	NA		NA
28	1,2,5,6	32	Low incorrect positives sent	NA	NA	30	34	NA		NA
29	1,2,5,6	29.5	Low total incorrect positives received	NA	NA	28	31	NA		NA

Study Number	Study Excluded	Study Averages	STUDY (All positives are for first and second requests, except Sauls-Bank.)	1 Davis, Neter, Palmer	2 Sauls Bank	3 Sauls Credit Union	4 Hubbard, Bullington	5 Warren Loan Accounts	(5,6)	6 Warren Share Accounts
30	1,2,5,6	92	% response low (29/28)	NA	NA	93	91	NA		NA
31	1,2,5,6	20.5	Low incorrect positives identified	NA	NA	25	16	NA		NA
32	1,2,5,6	69	% normal detection (31/29) low positive	NA	NA	89	52	NA		NA
33	1,2,5,6	64	% gross detection (31/28) low positive	NA	NA	83	47	NA		NA
34	1,2,5,6	31	% type II normal (29-31/29) low positive	NA	NA	11	48	NA		NA
35	1,2,5,6	36	% type II gross (28-31/31) low positive	NA	NA	17	53	NA		NA
36	5,6	36	% increase in response to second request (2-1/1)	34	47	29	33	NA		NA
37	4,5,6	30	Correct negatives sent	NA	NA	NA	34	27		28
38	4,5,6	7.67	Total correct negatives received	NA	NA	NA	14		9	
39	4,5,6	26	% response (38/37)	NA	NA	NA	41		16%	
40	4,5,6	0	Type I negatives received	NA	NA	NA	--	--	--	--
41	1,4,5,6	199	% type I negatives (40/38)	497	NA	NA	--	116	--	114
42	4,5,6	25.3	Incorrect negatives sent	NA	NA	NA	68		42	
43	4,5,6	26	Total incorrect negatives received	218	NA	NA	34		18	
44	4,5,6	71	% response (43/42)	43.9	NA	NA	50	20	39	19
45	1,4,5,6	35.7	Incorrect negatives identified	56.1	NA	NA	27	17	17	17
46	1,4,5,6	64.3	% normal detection (45/42)		NA	NA	40	83		83
47	4,5,6	13.0	% type II normal (42-45/42)	NA	NA	NA	60		7	
48	4,5,6	48.67	% type II irrational (43-45/43)	NA	NA	NA	21			
49	4,5,6	13.33	High incorrect negatives sent	NA	NA	NA	34	58		54**
50	4,5,6	27	High incorrect negatives identified	NA	NA	NA	15	13		12**
51	4,5,6	73	% normal detection high incorrect negatives (50/49)	NA	NA	NA	44	22		22
52	4,5,6	50.67	% type II normal (49-50/49) high negatives	NA	NA	NA	56	78		78
53	4,5,6	8.66	Low incorrect negatives sent	NA	NA	NA	34	58		60**
54	4,5,6	17	Low incorrect negatives identified	NA	NA	NA	12	7		7**
55	4,5,6	83	% normal detection (54/53) low incorrect negative	NA	NA	NA	35	12		12
56	4,5,6		% type II normal (53-54/53) low negative	NA	NA	NA	65	88		88
			Account mean $		@1500	3493	100	452		173
			Account median $		100	50		400		65
			Blank positive confirmation							
			% response		43	78				

*Incomplete

**Direction of high/low reversed

APPENDIX B

MEASURES USED IN THE STUDY

Definitions

Measures will now be developed to describe the study's results and quantify those errors that may occur with the use of the confirmation technique. See Exhibit B-1. It is assumed that information on the confirmation request agrees with the books, since this is common auditing practice. However, because this study deliberately introduced errors into the requests, an organization with incorrect books is known to be simulated in the study and therefore known to the auditor.

Recipient Behavior (Exhibit B-1)

In analyzing the responses to confirmation requests, the following major behaviors were observed.

The "responds and refuses task" category includes those respondents who returned the requests but refused to confirm or take exception to the information on the request. Examples are respondents who used the return envelope to request an address change, to request payoff data for the loan, or simply to inform the auditor that they did not desire to participate.

The "agrees with confirmation" respondents exhibited two basic behaviors.

First, some respondents simply agreed with the information on the request. For the positive format, only a signed reply was required. For the negative, agreement was signified whether or not a signed reply was received. For the expanded field, circling the correct amount and signing the reply constituted verification.[1]

The second type of behavior exhibited by "agrees with confirmation" respondents was the provision of sufficient information for an auditor to conclude that the organization's books were correct. For example, some respondents simply listed the payments made and/or the future payments to be made on the account. If the

Exhibit B-1
Derivation of Measures

Recipient Behavior	Organization's Books Are	
	Correct	Incorrect
Does not respond	A	E
Responds & refuses task	B	F
Agrees with confirmation	C	G
Correct about exception	Not possible	H
Incorrect about exception*	D	J

*A recipient may take exception to a confirmation and the auditor may still conclude that the books are not in error. For instance, a recipient may protest a penalty charge for a late payment on a loan although the charge is justified.

auditor believed the account balance to be correct after a comparison of the response with the books, the response was categorized as a verification.

The "correct about exception" group also displayed two similar respondent behaviors. First, respondents in this group took exception and the auditor, after comparing the response with the organization's books, concluded that the respondent was correct and the books were in error. Second, respondents furnished sufficient information on the response (such as the list of payments mentioned in the preceding paragraph) without formally taking an exception. If the information provided on the response resulted in an auditor's concluding that the books were erroneous, this type of response also was defined as a correct exception.

The "incorrect about exception" category also resulted from two respondent behaviors discussed previously. However, this category results from an auditor's conclusion that the organization, rather than the respondent, is correct.

NEW TYPES OF ERRORS WITH THE EXPANDED FIELD

Three new types of errors were found possible with the expanded field format.

In the first type of error, the information on the request may be correct, but the respondent may circle a wrong amount.[2] If the organization's books are correct, the auditor, by using alternative procedures, may conclude that the organization is correct and the respondent in error. This respondent behavior is defined as a Type I error.

The second type of error occurs when both the information on the expanded field request and the organization's books are erroneous and the respondent circles the amount that is shown on the books. This is defined as a verification, and is, therefore, a Type II error. This behavior is essentially the same as that which produces a Type II error when positives are sent and the books are incorrect.

The third new error occurs when the books are incorrect and the respondent circles one of the two amounts the auditor knows does not reflect the organization's booked amount for the account. For purposes of this analysis, circling the wrong signal or amount is classified as a detection. The rationale for this classification is an assumption that the auditor will, by alternative procedures, discover that the account is erroneously booked and hence detect the erroneous amount.[3]

ALGEBRA OF MEASURES

Although it may be argued that task refusers should be included in all the measures, this category was excluded primarily because a small survey of practitioners showed that typical assumptions about the behavior of nonrespondents and respondents who verify or take exception do not apply to task refusers.

For positives and the expanded fields, the following measures are used for the analysis of Exhibit B-1:

Response rate = $(C + D) / (A + C + D)$ or
$$(G + H + J) / (E + G + H + J)$$

Gross Type I error rate = $(D) / (A + C + D)$

Net Type I error rate = $(D) / (C + D)$

Gross Type II error rate = $(G + J) / (E + G + H + J)$

Net Type II error rate = $(G + J) / (G + H + J)$

Gross detection rate = $(H) / (E + G + H + J)$

Net detection rate = $(H) / (G + H + J)$

Task refusal rate = $(B) / (B + C + D)$ or $(F) / (F + G + H + J)$

Since the response rate for negatives is assumed to be 100%, net and gross rates for any one measure are identical. For negatives, the following measures are used:

Type II error rate = $(E + G + J) / (E + G + H + J)$

Detection rate = $(H) / (E + G + H + J)$

Task refusal rate = $(F) / (E + F + G + H + J)$

---

[1]For the discrepant expanded field, agreement was defined as circling the amount the auditor believed to be the booked amount even though, as a result of the simulation,

knowledge was available to the auditor that the circled amount was in error.

[2]One of the three amounts in the decision field should typically reflect the organization's books. When the respondent circles a wrong amount, the auditor will recognize erroneous respondent behavior.

[3]In a small survey of auditors, the consensus was that any response discrepancies must be reconciled when the auditor believes the books are correct. If it is assumed that the auditor is competent in the use of alternative procedures, it is reasonable to conclude that, in reconciling two erroneous data sets, the auditor will discover the inaccuracies in both sets. The actual effectiveness or reliability of the auditor under these circumstances might be worth further study.

APPENDIX C

THE IMPORTANCE OF THE STUDY AND SAMPLE SIZES

Because auditors rely on evidence to evaluate the accuracy of an organization's books, they are necessarily concerned with the quality of the evidence. Auditors are *effective* if they achieve the audit objectives. Auditors are *efficient* if the audit objectives are accomplished with as little effort (cost) as possible. This study is concerned with improving an auditing technique to increase its reliability. If reliability can be increased, auditors can perform their task more effectively and efficiently.

Reliability is defined as the degree to which audit evidence corresponds to an organization's books under the condition of accurate bookkeeping. If the books are inaccurate, then reliable audit evidence should result in the auditors' becoming aware of the inaccuracy. For example, if the instruments the auditors use to collect evidence are 100% reliable and the auditors are totally competent, then the auditors will be aware of all errors that are within the scope of their examination. But if the instruments are only 20% reliable, competent auditors would, on the average, be aware of only one-fifth of the errors that are within the scope of their examination.

Table C-1 illustrates the importance of improved reliability to the auditor.[1] It shows that if auditors use an instrument that is 90% reliable in detecting errors, they can be 90% confident of detecting one or more errors with a sample of approximately 2,350 (point A). If they use an instrument that is only 20% reliable, they can only be 39% confident of detecting one or more errors with the same sample size (point B). Thus, for a fixed sample size, auditors are less effective in detecting errors with the less reliable instrument.[2]

To be approximately 90% confident of detecting one or more errors with the 20% instrument, the auditor must sample the entire population of 10,000 (point C) or use a sample size more than four times as large as the sample size required for the same confidence level with the 90% reliable instrument. Therefore, under these circumstances, the more reliable instrument allows the auditors to be more efficient for a fixed confidence level because less effort (a smaller sample) is required. The following pages contain examples of other populations, defective rates or error rates, and instrument reliabilities.

---

[1]Appendix C resulted from a joint project undertaken by the author and Norton M. Holschuh, Department of Statistics, University of Minnesota, to develop a computer program for calculating probabilities accurate to three decimal places. The algorithm is based on the hypergeometric probability model and the recursive calculations required when the reliability of the instrument of measure is less than 1.000.

[2]The assumption is made that the costs for a fixed sample size are similar for either instrument.

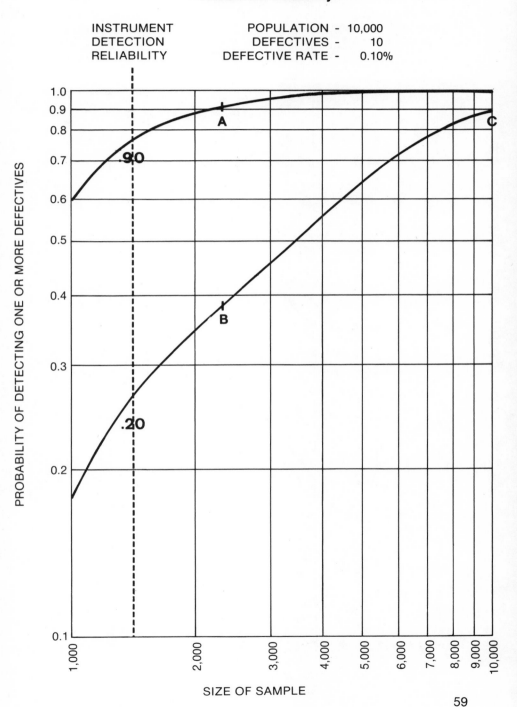

Table C-1
Detection Probability with Two Levels of
Instrument Reliability

INSTRUMENT   POPULATION - 10,000
DETECTION   DEFECTIVES -   10
RELIABILITY   DEFECTIVE RATE -   0.10%

PROBABILITY OF DETECTING ONE OR MORE DEFECTIVES

1.0
0.9
0.8
0.7
0.6
0.5
0.4
0.3
0.2
0.1

A

.90

B

.20

C

1,000 2,000 3,000 4,000 5,000 6,000 7,000 8,000 9,000 10,000

SIZE OF SAMPLE

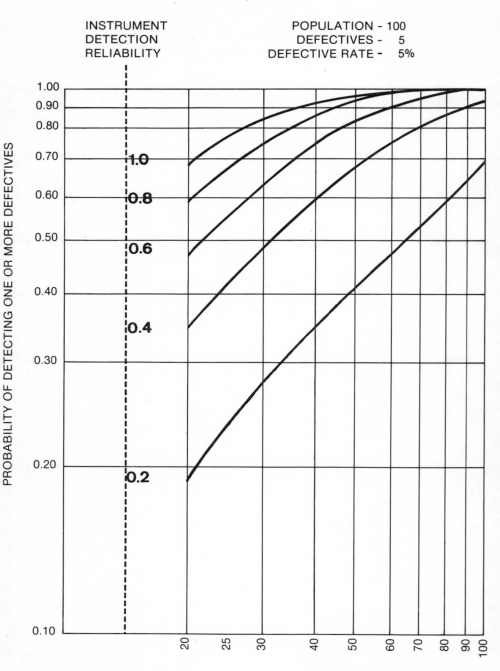

Table C-2
Detection Probability with Five Levels of Instrument Reliability
Example 1

INSTRUMENT
DETECTION
RELIABILITY

POPULATION - 100
DEFECTIVES - 5
DEFECTIVE RATE - 5%

PROBABILITY OF DETECTING ONE OR MORE DEFECTIVES

1.0
0.8
0.6
0.4
0.2

SIZE OF SAMPLE

Table C-2 (*continued*)
Example 2

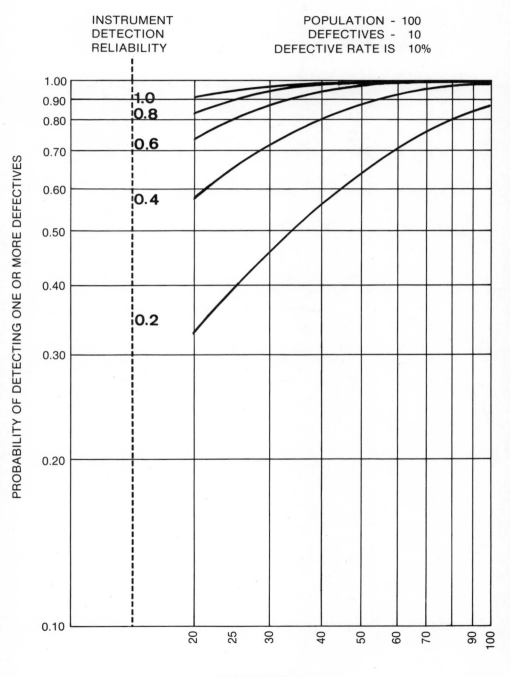

INSTRUMENT DETECTION RELIABILITY

POPULATION - 100
DEFECTIVES - 10
DEFECTIVE RATE IS 10%

PROBABILITY OF DETECTING ONE OR MORE DEFECTIVES

1.0
0.8
0.6
0.4
0.2

SIZE OF SAMPLE

Table C-2 (*continued*)
Example 3

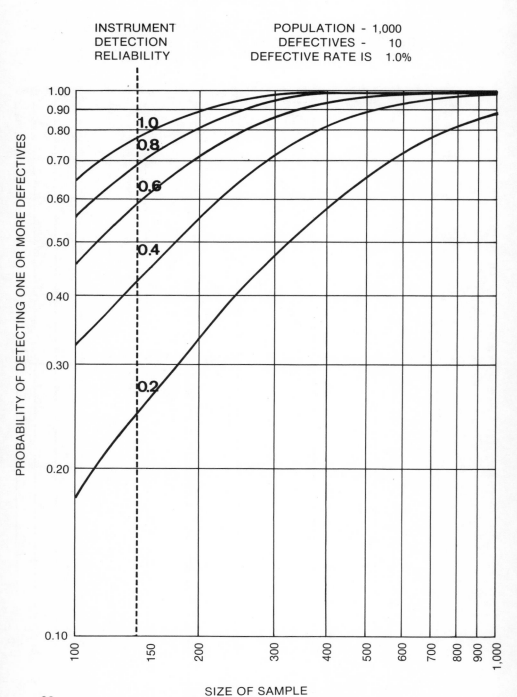

SIZE OF SAMPLE

Table C-2 (*continued*)
Example 4

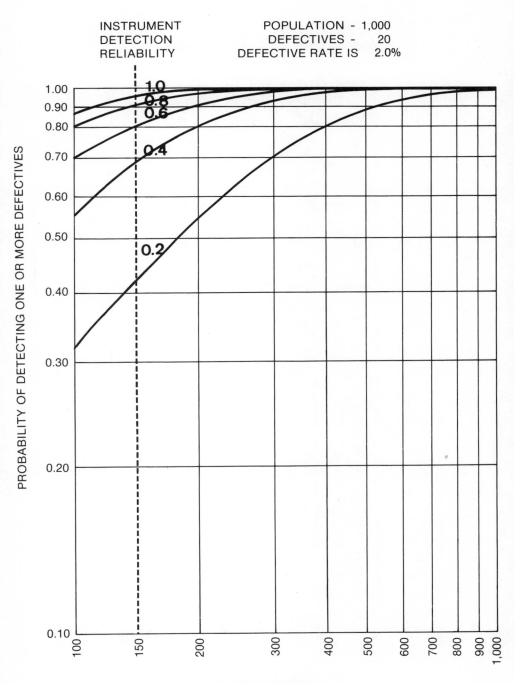

INSTRUMENT DETECTION RELIABILITY

POPULATION - 1,000
DEFECTIVES - 20
DEFECTIVE RATE IS 2.0%

PROBABILITY OF DETECTING ONE OR MORE DEFECTIVES

SIZE OF SAMPLE

Table C-2 (*continued*)
Example 5

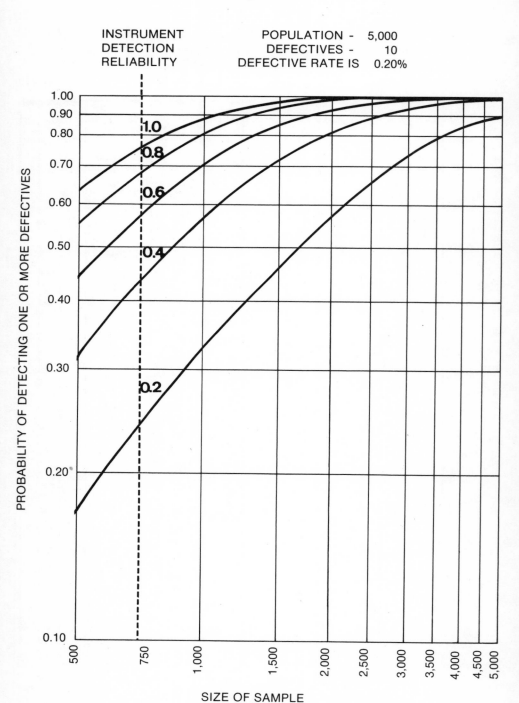

INSTRUMENT
DETECTION
RELIABILITY

POPULATION - 5,000
DEFECTIVES - 10
DEFECTIVE RATE IS 0.20%

PROBABILITY OF DETECTING ONE OR MORE DEFECTIVES

1.0
0.8
0.6
0.4
0.2

SIZE OF SAMPLE

Table C-2 (*continued*)
Example 6

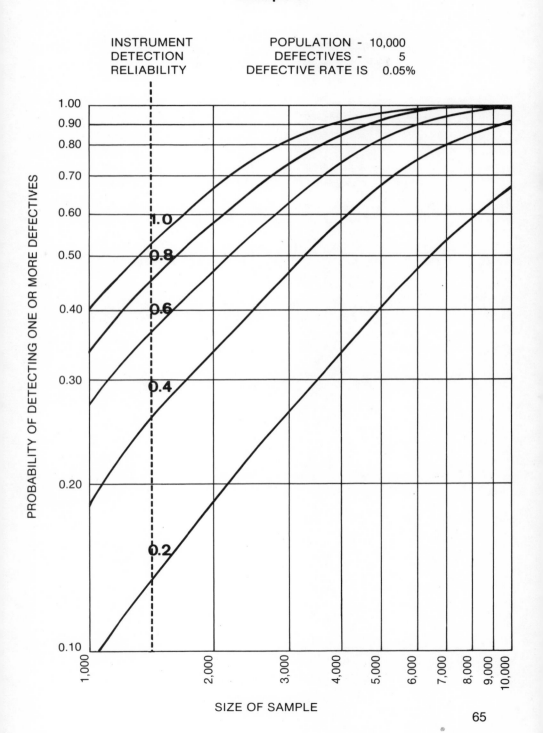

INSTRUMENT
DETECTION
RELIABILITY

POPULATION - 10,000
DEFECTIVES - 5
DEFECTIVE RATE IS 0.05%

PROBABILITY OF DETECTING ONE OR MORE DEFECTIVES

1.0
0.8
0.6
0.4
0.2

SIZE OF SAMPLE

65

SELECTED BIBLIOGRAPHY

American Accounting Association. *A Statement of Basic Auditing Concepts*. Sarasota, FL: American Accounting Association, 1973.

_____ . *A Statement of Basic Accounting Theory*. Evanston, IL: American Accounting Association, 1966.

American Institute of Accountants. *Statement on Auditing Procedure No. 1*. New York: American Institute of Accountants, 1939.

_____ . *Statement on Auditing Procedure No. 26*. New York: American Institute of Accountants, 1956.

_____ . *Statement on Auditing Procedure No. 33*. New York: American Institute of Accountants, 1963.

_____ . *Statement on Auditing Procedure No. 43*. New York: American Institute of Accountants, 1970.

American Institute of Certified Public Accountants. *Codification of Statements on Auditing Standards Numbers 1 to 7*. Chicago: Commerce Clearing House, 1976.

Anderson, R. J., and Leslie, Donald A. "Discussion of Considerations in Choosing Statistical Sampling Procedures in Auditing." *Journal of Accounting Research* (Supplement, 1975): 53-64.

Anderson, R. J., and Teitlebaum, A. D. "Dollar-Unit Sampling." *CA Magazine*, April 1973, pp. 30-39.

Arens, Alvin A., and Loebbecke, James K. *Auditing: An Integrated Approach*. Englewood Cliffs, NJ: Prentice-Hall, 1976.

Arkin, Herbert. *Handbook of Sampling for Auditing and Accounting*. New York: McGraw-Hill Book Co., 1963.

Canadian Institute of Chartered Accountants. *Confirmation of Accounts Receivable*. Toronto: Canadian Institute of Chartered Accountants, 1969.

Churchill, N. C., and Cooper, W. W. "Effects of Auditing Records: Individual Task Accomplishment and Organization Objectives." *New Perspective in Organization Research*, chap. xiv. Edited by W. W. Cooper, H. J. Leavitt, and M. W. Shelby. New York: John Wiley and Sons, 1964.

Davis, Gordon B.; Neter, John; and Palmer, Roger R. "An Experimental Study of Audit Confirmation." *Journal of Accounting*, June 1967, pp. 36-44.

Dicksee, Lawrence R. *Auditing: A Practical Manual for Auditors*. Authorized American ed. Edited by Robert H. Montgomery. New York: N. P., 1905.

Elliott, R., and Rogers, J. "Relating Statistical Sampling to Audit Objectives." *Journal of Accountancy*, June 1972, pp. 31-45.

Felix, William, Jr. "Discussion of Considerations in Choosing Statistical Sampling Procedures in Auditing." *Journal of Accounting Research* (Supplement, 1975): 65-67.

Felton, M. Robert. "The Problems with Direct Verification." *Magazine of Bank Administration*, November 1972, pp. 24-27.

Haseman, William D., and So, Yuk Ho. "An Information System Perspective of Computer Auditing." *Collected Papers of the American Accounting Association's Annual Meeting*. Sarasota, FL: American Accounting Association, 1976.

Holmes, Arthur W. *Auditing Principles and Procedures*. 6th ed. Homewood, IL: Richard D. Irwin, 1964.

Hubbard, Thomas D., and Bullington, Jerry B. "Positive and Negative Confirmation Requests — A Test." *Journal of Accounting*, March 1972, pp. 48-56.

Johnson, Arnold W. *Principles of Auditing*. New York: Rinehart, 1956.

Kaplan, Robert S. "Statistical Sampling in Auditing with Auxiliary Information Estimators." *Journal of Accounting Research* (Autumn 1973): 238-258.

Loebbecke, James K., and Neter, John. "Considerations in Choosing Statistical Sampling Procedures in Auditing." *Journal of Accounting Research* (Supplement, 1975): 38-52.

_____. "Statistical Sampling in Confirming Receivables." *Journal of Accountancy*, June 1973, pp. 44-50.

Magee, Robert P. "Discussion of Auditor's Loss Functions Implicit in Consumption-Investment Models." *Journal of Accounting Research* (Supplement, 1975): 121-123.

Mautz, R. K., and Sharaf, Hussein A. *Philosophy of Auditing*. Evanston, IL: American Accounting Association, 1961.

Meigs, Walter B.; Larsen, E. John; and Meigs, Robert F. *Principles of Auditing*. 5th ed. Homewood, IL: Richard D. Irwin, 1973.

Meikle, Giles B. *Statistical Sampling in an Audit Context*. Toronto: Canadian Institute of Chartered Accountants, 1972.

Moonitz, Maurice. *The Basic Postulates of Accounting*. New York: American Institute of Certified Public Accountants, 1961.

National Association for Bank Auditors and Comptrollers. *Customer Confirmation*. Park Ridge, IL: National Association for Bank Auditors and Comptrollers, 1967.

Neter, John. "Problems in Experimenting with the Application of Statistical Techniques in Auditing." *Accounting Review*, October 1954, pp. 581-600.

Newman, Benjamin. *Auditing a CPA Review Manual*. New York: John Wiley and Sons, 1958.

Palmer, Roger R.; Neter, John; and Davis, Gordon B. *A Research Study on the Effectiveness of Confirming Personal Checking Accounts*. Park Ridge, IL: National Association for Bank Auditors and Comptrollers, 1967.

Research Opportunities in Auditing. New York: Peat, Marwick, Mitchell & Co., 1976.

Sauls, Eugene H. "An Experiment on Nonsampling Errors." *Empirical Research in Accounting: Selected Studies*, pp. 157-171. Chicago: University of Chicago Press, 1971.

_____. "Nonsampling Errors in Accounts Receivable Confirmation." *Accounting Review*, January 1972, pp. 109-15.

Sorkin, Horton L. "An Empirical Study of Three Confirmation Techniques: Desirability of Expanding the Respondent's Decision Field." PhD dissertation, University of Minnesota, 1977.

Stettler, Howard F. *Auditing Principles.* 3rd ed. Englewood Cliffs, NJ: Prentice-Hall, 1970.

Vance, L., and Neter, John. *Statistical Sampling for Auditors and Accountants.* New York: John Wiley and Sons, 1956.

Warren, Carl S. "Selection Among Alternative Confirmation Forms." PhD dissertation, Michigan State University, 1973.

Watson, J. T. *To All Regional Administrators and National Bank Examiners.* Washington, DC: United States Treasury, February 1968.

Willingham, John J., and Carmichael, D. R. *Auditing Concepts and Methods.* New York: McGraw-Hill Book Co., 1971.

KILLERS ON THE MOUNTAIN

WILDERNESS FIRST AID AND LORE

SNAKEBITE

ACUTE MOUNTAIN SICKNESS

LIGHTNING

AVALANCHE

HYPOTHERMIA

WAYNE SMART, EMT

Library of Congress Control Number: 2021942609

ISBN: 978-1-7372762-1-0

Armin Lear Press Inc
215 W Riverside Drive, #4362
Estes Park, CO 80517

FOREWORD

This is a book about some bad things that can happen to you in the mountains—things that can kill you, in fact.

Other books covering wilderness first aid usually hit only the high points. For those who want a deeper understanding, such as Search and Rescue team members, this book contains a wider range of information on each subject.

And for information junkies who are looking for even more detail, the sources of all materials are found in the notes.

TABLE OF CONTENTS

CHAPTER 1- SNAKEBITE

CHAPTER 2 - ACUTE MOUNTAIN ILLNESS

CHAPTER 3 - LIGHTNING

CHAPTER 4 - AVALANCHE

CHAPTER 5 - HYPOTHERMIA

— CHAPTER 1 —

SNAKEBITE

On October 7, 2017, a 31-year-old Ironman triathlete was hiking with a friend outside Golden, Colorado. They were about a mile and a half from the trailhead on Mt. Galbraith when suddenly and without warning he was bitten on the ankle by a rattlesnake. His friend immediately called 911. Rescuers arrived a short 22 minutes later and evacuated the man to a waiting ambulance. He was taken to a hospital only ten minutes away. Despite heroic efforts by the emergency room staff he died a few hours later of heart failure.[1]

VENOMOUS SNAKES IN THE MOUNTAINS IN THE UNITED STATES

RATTLESNAKES

This unfortunate hiker was bitten by a prairie rattlesnake, also known as a western rattlesnake, the only kind of venomous snakes found in the mountains of Colorado. Other rattlesnakes such as the western diamondback are also found in mountainous areas in the United States.[2] Rattlesnakes are referred to as *crotaline snakes* or *pit vipers* from the small **heat-seeking organ** in a pit-like depression behind each nostril. This organ allows the snake, which has poor eyesight, to "see" infrared heat from the bodies of humans and warm-blooded animals.

Prairie Rattlesnake

Rattlesnakes also have an exceptionally keen **sense of smell**. They can sense olfactory stimuli both through their nostrils and by flicking their tongues.[3]

Crotaline venom is *cytotoxic;* it causes tissue damage in the area of the snakebite as well as systemic damage in other parts of the body. It is also *hemotoxic;* it damages the blood and blood vessels which ultimately can lead to death if the victim is not immediately transported and treated.

Rattlesnakes have two curved fangs which are retractable and lay against the roof of the mouth when the snake is not striking. Each snake has at least three pairs of replacement fangs.[4] Baby rattlesnakes are toxic as soon as they are born.[5]

Rattlesnakes can be identified by several physical characteristics. A rattlesnake's head is triangular and broader than its neck because of the large venom glands on the side of its upper jaw. They have **thick bodies** whereas non-venomous snakes do not have triangular heads and, with rare exceptions, are lithe and slender. If you can see the slits, you are dangerously close to the snake.

ARIZONA CORAL SNAKES

Another kind of venomous snake that can also be found in the mountains in the United States is the **Arizona coral snake**. Coral snakes are *viperid* snakes, and their venom is *neurotoxic*. It mostly affects the nerves, including those which regulate your breathing and heartbeat. Ultimately a shutdown of those nerves will lead to death. However, no deaths have been reported from bites of this snake.[6]

Arizona coral snakes are slender and small—13 to 21 inches. They have broad alternating bands of red and black separated by narrower bands of bright white or yellow. The bands encircle the body. The head is black, and the snout is blunt.[7]

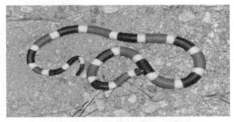
Arizona Coral Snake

Coral snakes have the second-strongest venom—the black mamba is first—but they are generally considered less dangerous than rattlesnakes because they have a less effective poison delivery system. They have a pair of small, hollow fangs for delivering their venom, however, unlike the rattlesnake, coral snakes' fangs are fixed in position in the front of the mouth. Coral snake fangs are small and not very efficient at delivering venom. As a result, coral snakes don't strike quickly like a rattlesnake. Instead, they bite with a chewing motion to inject more venom. [8]

When frightened or provoked, a coral snake will hide its head under its body and raise its tail, which looks like its head, and expel air from its *cloaca*—an orifice for the urinary, reproductive, and intestinal tract—making a popping noise, to scare off predators and other threats.[9] Predictably, these "micro-farts" have a very unpleasant smell.[10]

Because of the coral snake's dangerous reputation, many nonpoisonous snakes disguise themselves as coral snakes by having similar body patterns. To distinguish coral snakes from the harmless variety, some people memorize a little rhyme:

"Red on yellow, unhappy fellow,

Red on black, friend of Jack"[11]

The best advice is to **stay away from all snakes** that look anything like a coral snake.

INCIDENCE OF SNAKEBITE IN THE UNITED STATES

Over 9,000 people seek medical help for snakebites in the United States each year and five die. Separate figures are not kept for those bitten in the mountains.[12]

LOCATION AND PREFERRED HABITAT OF SNAKES

RATTLESNAKES

Rattlesnakes are found in all parts of the mountains, but usually not above 9,500 feet – probably because of the lack of prey and the colder, wetter climate for much of the year. However, they have been seen as high as 13,000 feet.[13]

As a general rule, rattlesnakes like an ambient temperature of 60 degrees or more[14]. This is somewhat misleading in that a snake can feel much warmer coiled up on a flat rock in the sun. Snakes are more active and out sunning themselves on the trail in the mornings and evenings. During the heat of the day, they are more likely to be hiding under rocks or in the grass or foliage by a trail where they can be threatened by someone's passing and strike.

ARIZONA CORAL SNAKES

Arizona coral snakes are found in arid and semiarid regions in numerous habitats, both on plans and on lower mountain slopes up to 5,800 feet (1,768 meters). In Arizona they are especially numerous in rocky, upland desert.[15]

They are usually nocturnal or crepuscular (appearing at twilight). [16]

BRUMATION (HIBERNATION) PATTERNS

RATTLESNAKES

Rattlesnakes may be encountered generally from April through October.[17] In other months they are said to be in *brumnation*, as opposed to hibernation, that is, "a state or condition of sluggishness, inactivity, or torpor exhibited by reptiles during winter or extended periods of low temperature."[18] Research has shown that the number of snakebites is less following drought and more following precipitation. [19]

ARIZONA CORAL SNAKES

Arizona coral snakes, being in a warmer climate, are active a little longer, from March to November, after which they go into brumation.[20]

AVOIDING RATTLESNAKES

The best ways to avoid getting bitten by a venomous snake are:

- Stay on the trail.
- Don't let children wander onto the edge of the trail.
- Avoid walking in tall grass or thick shrubbery.
- Watch where you put your hands.
- When stepping off the trail to answer the call of nature, scan the ground around you.
- Keep dogs on a leash.
- Keep your eyes on the trail ahead.
- Carry a flashlight to see the snake, but especially his eyes, which shine red in the reflection.
- Keep one ear bud out if listening to music.
- When stepping out of the car in the trailhead parking lot, keep an eye out for snakes.
- Look before you sit.
- Don't run over snakes in your vehicle if you can safely avoid it. The snake may become entangled in your engine compartment or undercarriage and greet you later on, wounded but still lethal.
- Probe ahead with a walking stick before entering an area with an obscured view of your feet.
- Do not sleep in the open or in poorly sealed accommodations in areas where snakes are common.
- Check sleeping bag, boots, and other equipment before use.
- **Do not pick up snakes** even when you think they are dead.

ENCOUNTERS WITH SNAKES

Snakes "hear" you through the vibrations caused by your feet as you walk nearby. Making loud noises doesn't help. Snakes have no ears and can't hear in the sense that humans and other mammals hear, but vibration from your footsteps or striking the ground with a walking stick or trekking poles might create enough vibration to warn of your arrival.[21]

Crotaline snakes are not aggressive but will strike if they feel threatened.

Do not try to pick up a snake! Assume all snakes are poisonous, and do not approach them.

A television show several years ago starring Australian Steve Irwin as *The Crocodile Hunter* regularly pictured him picking up black mambas—neurotoxic snakes—and other poisonous snakes by the tail. Steve was later stung and killed while swimming too close to a large manta ray.[22] The point being, stay away from things that can kill you, like rattlesnakes.

If a snake is not within striking distance, that is, 1/2 to 2/3 of its length, freeze and slowly back away.[23] If the snake is closer, and you are afraid it will strike if you move, you can have someone else shield you by holding a jacket, hat or shirt between you and the snake using a branch or trekking poles, as you slowly back off.

Don't assume that every rattlesnake will give you fair warning of its presence. They don't always shake their rattles before striking. A snake's rattle is fragile and easily broken. As a result the snake may not be able to make enough noise to be heard.

SNAKES IN GROUPS

RATTLESNAKES

Rattlesnakes typically live as solitary animals and hunt alone. If you see them together, they are probably a mother with her young, particularly in the autumn, or two snakes mating. However, sometimes snakes will share resting places, such as on a sunny ledge together during cold months. So, if you see one snake, be sure to look around for others in the area.

"JUMPING" OR "LAUNCHING" SNAKES

Stories abound about snakes jumping or launching themselves at a hiker. Experts will tell you that a snake can do neither.[24] When threatened, a snake will coil itself up to present a smaller target to predators and to stage itself for a strike which will be between 1/2 and 2/3 of its length.[25] However if a snake strikes downhill, its momentum may carry it farther forward than would occur over flat ground. On very steep slopes, a snake could lose balance during a strike and actually fall towards its target.

PATHWAY OF VENOM IN THE BODY: RATTLESNAKES

"Venom injected by a snakebite disperses away from the injection site by a variety of mechanisms that are a function of venom biochemistry (the size of the venom molecules), site anatomy (where the bite occurs), and of deliberate and inadvertent secondary processes such as limb position (raised or lowered arm), muscle activity (walking) and first aid activities (compression bandages, etc.)"[26]

Generally, snake venom may enter the body in three ways:

1. Venom injected directly into a vein during a snakebite

Venom may be injected directly into a vein, for example, into the veins on the back of the hand, arm, head, foot, or ankle. In these cases, the venom immediately enters the blood system and will do a complete circuit of the body in less than a minute, depending on how fast the victim's heart is beating. There is nothing that can be done to interrupt this circulation in time to be effective.

2. Venom that enters the victim through a cut or crack in the skin.

Extended Fangs of a Rattlesnake

In the past, treatment for snakebite called for the rescuer to cut a small "x" across the injection site and suck the venom out. This often resulted in envenomation of the rescuer through small fissures around the teeth from *gingivitis,* through sores in the mouth, or through cracks in the lips of the rescuer. This protocol was not effective in removing the venom in any case. As such it has long since been discarded as a viable method of treatment. [27]

It follows that venom can enter the body through any other cut or crack in the skin, such as an open hangnail.

3. Pit viper (rattlesnake) venom injected into the intercellular space and collected by the lymph system

Most, if not all, of the pit viper venom is injected into the *intercellular space*— the space between the cells—at the capillary level. In almost all cases the venom molecules of pit vipers are too large to enter the venous blood capillaries there. Instead they are absorbed by the body's *lymph system* and ultimately conveyed to the *lymph ducts,* dumped into the blood system and carried to the organs where they do most of their damage.[28] The venom also can damage the lymph vessels and blood vessels on the way and affect the ability of the blood to coagulate.

Lymph from the upper right quadrant of the body ultimately arrives at the *right lymphatic duct* where it is dumped into the *right subclavian vein.* Lymph from the rest of the body travels to the *thoracic duct* where it is dumped into the *left subclavian vein.* It is important to note that the two lymph systems are not connected.

Movement of the *lymph fluid* in the lymph vessels is accomplished by (1) the squeezing action of smooth muscles in the walls of the *lymphangions,* the lymph vessels,[29] [30] (2) changes in thoracic pressure from breathing,[31] (3) arterial pressure from adjacent arteries,[32] and (4) muscular contraction such as the kind that occurs during walking.

From this we see that movement of the venom through the lymph system can be hastened indirectly by increasing the victim's heart rate and rate of respiration and by muscular contraction. Thus, walking back to the trailhead is problematical if it has the effect of increasing lymph flow from arterial pressure, respiratory pressure, and muscle pressure.[33] This is the reason for the standard protocol which is to **immobilize and transport.**

An exception to the standard protocol is when a person is bitten in the right hand or arm. As noted above, the lymph system in the upper right quadrant of the body is independent of the lymph system for the rest of the body, including the legs. The two systems are not connected. Therefore, the squeezing action of the lymphangions in the rest of the body and the muscular contraction in the legs from walking will not increase the rate of squeezing of the lymphangions in the upper right quadrant where the bite is. The victim's heart rate and breathing will undoubtedly already be elevated from anxiety over the snakebite. So as long as the victim's heart rate and respiration from walking are not higher than that already caused by his anxiety over the snakebite, there is no harm in starting to walk out to meet the rescue crew.

Although the lymph system is similar to the circulatory system, it operates much slower, and it could be an hour or even longer before pit viper venom reaches a lymph duct, is dumped into the blood stream and gets to vital organs. Optimizing the use of this hour could be crucial in getting the victim to a hospital and treating the effects of the venom.

Following are several YouTube presentations discussing the operation of the lymph system:

The Lymphatic System—Lymph Nodes, Medicosis Perfectionalist, September 26, 2018

The Lymphatic System—All You Need to Know, September 22, 2018

The Lymphatic System, Ray Cinti, February 3, 2014

The Lymphatic System: Crash Course A&P #44, November 30, 2015

Introduction to the Lymphatic System, June 21, 2017

PATHWAY OF VENOM IN THE BODY—
ARIZONA CORAL SNAKE

The pathway of venom from an Arizona coral snake in the body is mostly different from that of a rattlesnake. Because the venom molecules of an Arizona coral snake are smaller, they can be taken up by the blood capillaries at the site of the wound. From there the venom is transferred to the rest of the venous system and thence to the organs of the body where they do their damage.[34] Obviously without intervention, such as a pressure bandage, this happens much faster than evacuation of the venom through the lymph system.

EFFECTS OF ENVENOMATION ON THE BODY

Twenty percent of snake bites are "dry" and do not result in envenomation[35] (but see **Delayed Symptoms** and **Recurrence of Symptoms** below). The amount of venom in a bite may vary substantially.[36] Young snakes who haven't had much practice may empty their entire venom gland into the victim. These are the most dangerous bites.

Crotaline snakes in Colorado have both *hemotoxic venom* and *cytotoxic venom*[37] which have the following effects:

- *Local tissue effects* – pain, soft tissue *necrosis* (death), inflammation, swelling, redness, and tenderness which spread with the movement of the venom through the lymph system
- *Effects on blood* — degradation of blood components
- *Systemic effects* — low blood pressure, nausea and vomiting, and failure of organ function

TECHNO-SPEAK: For readers who want more detailed information, following is a summary of the **toxic effects of crotaline venom** as provided by the Journal of the Wilderness Medical Society:[38]

Snake venoms contain many enzymes and other toxins that disrupt cellular processes, resulting in vascular damage and tissue destruction. This results in tissue loss and release of potassium into the circulation. If potassium levels rise high enough (*hyperkalemia*), this will cause heart irregularities (*dysrhythmias*). Muscle destruction also releases protein (*myoglobin*) into the circulation, and this can result in kidney damage (*acute renal failure*). Vascular damage allows leakage of fluid into the tissues, resulting in *peripheral edema* (swelling of the legs and ankles), *pulmonary edema* (fluid in the lungs), *hypovolemia,* (decreased blood volume) caused by plasma leaving the veins and flooding the legs and lungs, and *metabolic acidosis* (excessive quantities of acid in the body). Other toxins disrupt the *coagulation processes*. For example, some toxins promote *coagulation* and result in *diffuse intravascular clotting* that can, rarely, result in heart attacks or strokes. More commonly, snake venoms result in the degradation of blood-clotting factors, and may result in the opposite effect, blood which will not coagulate and excessive bleeding at essentially any site, e.g., intracranial bleeding around the brain.

INITIAL SIGNS AND SYMPTOMS OF A RATTLESNAKE BITE

Expect to see one or two **fang marks** (or more if the snake strikes more than once) from both rattlesnakes and Arizona coral snakes.

In addition, the victim or a rattlesnake bite can experience one or more of the following from a snakebite:

- **Localized pain** which can become quite severe
- **Bruising**
- **Redness** from inflammation
- **Streaking** representing lymph ducts which became inflamed from carrying venom[39]
- **Blistering**
- **Swelling** around the bite; also as the venom progresses throughout the body swelling may develop around the trachea in which case rescue breathing may be required to keep the victim's airway open. Note: Only about 1 percent of snakebites are on the **head or neck**, but these involve a high risk of subsequent loss of airway
- **Nausea**
- **Numbness**
- *Anaphylaxis* (a severe allergic reaction causing dilation of the blood vessels) - in these cases the victim's EpiPen should be administered if she has one. If no EpiPen is available, give the victim two or three Benadryl capsules and instruct her to bite down on them to release the liquid inside. For best effect the liquid should be held for several minutes *sublingual* (under the tongue) where there is abundant vascularization allowing for rapid infusion of the Benadryl into the body. After a couple of minutes the liquid can be swallowed with a sip of water. Benadryl tablets can be chewed up by the victim at which point salivation will occur, and similarly held under the tongue. The generic name of Benadryl is diphenhydramine
- **Swelling of lymph nodes** in the groin or armpit within an hour if the bite is on the leg or arm[40]

Also expect to see **intense anxiety**, and at times, **panic attack** and an acute sense of **impending doom.**[41] It follows that the victim's **pulse** and **respiration** will be heightened.

Keep in mind that envenomation is a **"dynamic disease state,"** also known as a **"progressive disorder,"** meaning that the foregoing symptoms may present serially, i.e., one after another, as the effects of the venom advance through the victim.[42]

DELAYED APPEARANCE OF SYMPTOMS

In some snakebites, symptoms do not appear immediately. Thus, in the case of apparent dry bites, the victim should be monitored for several hours.[43]

RECURRENCE OF SYMPTOMS

In some cases, after treatment with antivenoms, local and *systemic recurrences* (worsening after initial improvement) have been observed. This may result in greater tissue injury and negative effects on the blood—*hemotoxic recurrence*—which may result in the risk of hemorrhage. The latter is of particular concern because hemotoxic recurrence usually occurs after the patient is discharged from the hospital. [44]

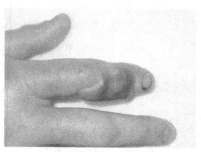

Snakebite on Hand

INITIAL SIGNS AND SYMPTOMS OF AN ARIZONA CORAL SNAKEBITE

There is usually only mild pain associated with a bite.[45]

VARIABLES AFFECTING THE TOXIC EFFECTS OF A SNAKEBITE

The toxic effects of a snakebite depend on:

- The age of the victim—children and older people are more at risk
- The health of the victim
- The age of the snake—young snakes are more likely to inject all of their venom in a single bite
- The size of the victim

- The amount of venom injected
- The location of the bite such as bites into veins, for example, on the back of the hand; bites on the face or neck are more dangerous
- The number of bites—a snake may strike twice within a second

PEDIATRIC SNAKEBITES

Children are at risk for snakebites because they frequently play outdoors and often reach or step into areas blindly. Snakebites among children are more serious if only because of a child's smaller size.[46]

SNAKEBITE AND THE ELDERLY

Snakebite in the elderly is somewhat different than snakebite in younger victims. This is because the elderly often have weaker immune responses and suffer from other *morbidities* (diseases) for which they are taking medications that can interfere with their blood clotting response.[47]

SNAKEBITE DURING PREGNANCY

Snakebite in pregnant women is more dangerous because they tend to have lower blood pressure than normal, which can be further diminished by snake venom.[48] In addition, having a pregnant woman lie on her back during evacuation can cause *supine hypotensive syndrome*, with further lowering of blood pressure due to the weight of the fetus on the blood vessels running to and from the heart. Thus, a pregnant snakebite victim who is transported by stretcher should lie on her (preferably left) side or sit upright.[49]

Unfortunately, the placenta is not a barrier to the systemic effects of envenomation, and a snakebite can cause significant adverse effects in the fetus, including miscarriage.[50] Safe, rapid transport to a hospital is indicated in any snakebite of a pregnant woman, even if the bite appears to be dry (see Delayed Reactions above).

PROTECTION FROM SNAKEBITE

Boots – Snakebites on the ankle are common. The recent victim in Golden was bitten on the ankle, as was a woman in Colorado Springs the same year. Although hiking or running shoes are commonly worn for hiking, they don't offer as much protection as hiking boots. Hiking sandals or flip-flops offer almost no protection and should be avoided. The same is true of going barefoot.[51] Tall rubber wading boots provide the best protection, especially in tall grass or brush where snakes may lie hidden.

Long pants and Leg gaiters – Long pants particularly if they are loose or baggy, and leg gaiters may offer some protection from leg bites.[52] Shorts are comfortable, cool and stylish, but they leave your leg bare and more vulnerable to a serious bite.

"DEAD" SNAKES

The old saw, "A snake never dies until sundown,'" has more than a little truth. Even after suffering potentially fatal injuries and being presumed dead, venomous snakes have a reflex bite action and are capable of injuring humans.[53] This happens because the snake's heat sensory pits are active until rigor mortis sets in.[54] Consider these snakebite stories reported by two doctors in Phoenix, Arizona:

- "Patient 1 shot a rattlesnake, striking its head several times and observed no movement for three minutes. When he picked the snake up, it envenomed his right index finger.
- Patient 2 shot and then decapitated a rattlesnake. When he picked up the head, his index finger was envenomed.
- Patient 3 was envenomed in his left ring finger and right index finger by a decapitated rattlesnake head that had been motionless for five minutes.
- Patient 4 was envenomed on his index finger by a rattlesnake he presumed to be dead from multiple gunshot wounds, including one to the head."[55]

Clearly the only safe course of action when you think you have killed a snake is to leave it where it is.

TREATMENT OF A CROTALINE (PIT VIPER) SNAKEBITE

In general, the treatment protocol for a crotaline snakebite is 'immobilize and transport,' which means sit the victim down in a safe place and wait for the local rescue to come and carry him to the trailhead.

In more detail, your response to a snake bite should look like this:

- First of all, **protect** the victim from another bite, as stated above, and then **move** her away from the last seen location of the snake and try to **calm** her.

- If the snake is still visible, quickly **take a picture** or pictures of it on your cellphone, being careful not to get within striking range, to show to the doctors in the emergency room. If you are not able to take a picture of the snake, **do not wash the area of the bite.** It is important to retain traces of the venom on the skin which medical staff may capture by swabbing.[56]

- **Do not attempt to kill the snake.** It is illegal to kill a snake in many states unless it is threatening your life or property, and snakes are difficult to kill anyhow. You are likely to get bitten, and your efforts to kill the snake delay the victim's arrival at the hospital. Also keep in mind that snakes are an important part of the ecosystem, and it is unethical to kill an animal which is just defending itself and is no longer a threat to you. In addition, shooting a snake may violate local laws against discharging firearms in a populated area.[57]

- As soon as you see signs that the snakebite is not dry, **leave a message** on your SPOT satellite unit or **call for help** on your cellphone, if you are within range. Describe your location, details about the victim and her symptoms, and resources at hand. If you are not within cellphone range, **send for help.** For safety's sake, it is always best to send two people, rather than one alone, with adequate supplies and survival gear to protect themselves and a map showing the location of the victim.

- **Remove** all rings, watches, bracelets or piercings on the extremity in anticipation of swelling. If the bite is near a shoe or boot, remove it also since swelling inside a shoe or boot can cause pain and restrict blood flow. Protect the foot from cold weather.

- Except as stated above, wipe the fang marks with an **antiseptic wipe.** Then **draw a circle** around them with a ballpoint pen or marker and the time of the bite. Continue to draw circles around the swelling with the time every half hour or so to keep track of the progress of the envenomation.[58]

- Cover the fang marks with a **loose sterile dressing.**

- Apply a **pressure bandage or** a **cold pack** if you anticipate a long delay in arriving at the hospital, and you want to slow down the onset of systemic reactions, or the snakebite is by an elapid, such as a coral snake.

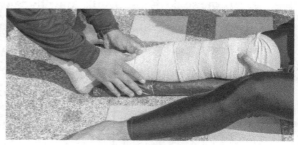

Pressure Bandage

- **Immobilize** the bitten extremity with a splint and/or sling. Any movement or muscular contraction in the extremity increases absorption of the venom into the lymph system and ultimately the bloodstream.[59]

- Administer a **pain killer** such as acetaminophen. Do not give the victim anti-inflammatories such as aspirin or ibuprofen since they may interfere with the body's response to the venom. Opioids, such as Vicodin, are also appropriate, if the victim has them, since they work only on the nervous system.[60]

- For snakebites on an arm or leg, there is no consensus whether to elevate the affected extremity or not. Those advocating the former[61] [62] contend that it is better to let gravity help drain the venom from the wound site and thereby minimize local damage. Those in favor of not elevating the wound[63] are more concerned with the systemic effects the venom can have on the rest of the body, including the possibility of death. I have found no clinical research showing that raising or lowering the extremity has any measurable effect on the lymph flow in any event.

- Ask others coming by on the trail to **stay and help** in case you have to carry the victim out or administer CPR.

- Immediately begin treating for **shock.** If you wait until you think you see signs of shock, you will be too late. Treatment consists of:

  - Dealing with the **underlying pathology**, that is, the snakebite.

- Putting the victim in a **position of comfort**. Ash her how she is most comfortable. Don't assume that lying flat is the best position. Older people and individuals with scoliosis may not be able to lie flat. (Also see Snakebite and Pregnancy above). Many victims feel disempowered, embarrassed and/or claustrophobic when lying down.

- Maintaining the victim's **body temperature**. In Colorado, for example, that might mean keeping the victim cool during the day and warm at night.

- Keeping the **victim dry**. Water conducts heat 100 times faster than air.

- **Reassuring the victim**. It is extremely important to stay calm and reassure the victim. This is a continuing part of the rescue protocol, particularly as the effects of the envenomation become more obvious to the victim.

DO NOT:

Make **cuts** over the fang marks and try to suck the venom out by mouth. It is ineffective and harmful to the victim and may possibly poison the rescuer.[64]

DO NOT:

Apply an **electrical shock** on the fang marks using a car battery or stun gun. This is an urban myth and is totally ineffective and may cause damage to the tissue and even induce cardiac arrest.[65]

In 1990, the US Food and Drug Administration banned the promotion of electrical devices on the grounds that they had no therapeutic value in the treatment of snakebite.[66]

DO NOT:

Apply a **tourniquet** above the wound; it can lead to retention of venom and tissue damage through *ischemia* (low or no blood flow) and *necrosis* (death) of the flesh around the wound.[67] Also, application of a tourniquet frequently complicates wound progression by delaying clearance of venom from the affected area.[68] In addition, a tight tourniquet left on too long can ultimately cause gangrene and result in amputation of the extremity.[69]

Note: *Elapid* snakes, such as the Arizona coral snake found in the southern United States, have **neurotoxic venom,** which affects the nervous system and the brain. Early tourniquet administration or pressure bandages may delay toxic effects in these cases.[70]

PRESSURE BANDAGES

Pressure bandages and immobilization (PBI) are used in Australia where most of the snakes are elapids, that is, *neurotoxic,* and it is important to slow the movement of venom in the vascular system. Unlike the tourniquet, PBI does not cause major *ischemia* —blood deprivation—in the extremity and is safe for humans. It is based on applying a bandage at pressures of about 60 mmHg, which is below the *diastolic pressure,* that is, the pressure for deep arterial blood flow, but above that for lymphatic flow. Pressure bandages are difficult to apply correctly in the field, even for professionals. Use of a **blood pressure cuff** is one way of accurately gauging the right pressure.[71] BPI can be used for Arizona coral snakebites in the southern United States. Elapid venom is primarily neurotoxic and causes limited local damage. BPI can also be used when you want to delay movement of the venom in the lymph system for other reasons, for example to delay lymph flow because the hospital is a long way away.

Arizona coral snake venom typically causes little pain at the site of the bite.[72]

DO NOT:

Apply *cryotherapy* using cold packs or chemical freezing devices such as wart removers. Initial exposure to cold temperatures on the skin activates thermoregulatory mechanisms and causes vasodilation, which increases blood flow and may contribute to the spreading of the venom. As tissues are further cooled, vasoconstriction occurs which limits blood flow and can cause localized damage around the bite, including frostbite.[73]

APPLICATION OF COLD

Notwithstanding the foregoing, there may be instances in which the victim and the rescuer want to slow down the rate of flow in the lymph system after a pit viper bite, even though it may increase damage to the flesh at the site of the bite. In such cases, cooling the affected limb with ice or cold packs has been shown to approximately halve the rate of lymph flow, and thus delay the time when systemic effects are felt. Ice should not be applied directly to the skin. Use a sock or other cloth.

DO NOT:

Give the victim an alcoholic drink as an antidote.[74] Alcohol has been given to snakebite victims in the belief that venom and alcohol are antagonists and will neutralize each other. There is no science supporting this practice. Similarly, there is no evidence that a snakebite will have no effect on a person who is already inebriated.

Alcoholic beverages have been used in snakebite cases to take the victim's mind off the situation, however, alcohol can mask other symptoms. Also, alcohol acts as a vasodilator and may hasten the spread of the venom.

DO NOT:

Give the victim **food or drink** unless transport times are long in which case you can allow the victim to take clear liquids, but no solids, as long as there is no nausea or vomiting.

MECHANICAL VENOM EXTRACTORS

Various commercial snakebite venom extractors are available for purchase. These products are designed to draw venom from the snakebite wound and ostensibly lessen or eliminate the effects of the venom. Researchers and medical personnel almost unanimously advise against this practice on the grounds that it is ineffective, the venom already having been dispersed into the body, and will result in a harmful loss of blood leading to tissue death and lesions around the bite.[75]

For obvious reasons, it is not possible to experiment on humans with extraction of live venom. Venom extraction experiments have, however, been tried on pigs, which have skin similar to human skin, but did not result in a significant removal of venom.[76] Reports of these experiments did not reveal how long after envenomation the extractor was applied.

In another experiment, a mock venom was injected into a human volunteer's leg. An extractor pump was applied three minutes after injection. The post extraction count revealed less than a 2 percent decrease in the total body venom load.[77]

In view of the present state of research, use of a venom extractor is not recommended.

USE OF BOTANICALS IN TREATING SNAKEBITE

Although botanicals have commonly been used in treating snakebite around the world, no plant remedy has been systematically proven to have a beneficial effect on snakebite envenomation in humans. Some studies have hinted at the presence of components in botanicals that may have therapeutic benefits for the treatment of snakebite, but no clinical study to date has shown an improvement of outcome in patients treated with a specific plant.[78]

PHARMACEUTICAL INHIBITION OF LYMPH FLOW

Topical agents to inhibit lymph flow have been reported in the literature, including Rectogesic, a nitric oxide agent, which is commercially available. These would be useful in elapid snakebites, and in instances where delay in getting the victim of a pit viper bite to the hospital is anticipated.[79]

SCARIFICTION, INCISION AND AMPUTATION

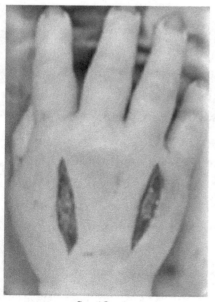

Scarification

Enlarging the snakebite wound by making cuts around it to increase bleeding and elimination of venom is known as "scarification." Currently the practice is considered archaic and may result in introduction of venom remaining on the victim's skin, as well as possible infection.[80]

The most extreme form of incision is amputation of a finger or toe. Not only does this have permanent consequences, but it is not necessary in the case of dry bites and is probably ineffective due to the rapid dissemination of venom in the victim.

SNAKE STONES

Snake stones are stones or pieces of charred bone that are applied to a snakebite site. It is claimed that they will absorb all of the venom. Although this practice is still carried on in parts of the world snakestones are not effective.[81]

CAUTERIZATIONS

Cauterization—**applying high heat** to the snakebite—has been used over the millennia to stop bleeding and sterilize a wound, or in the case of snakebites, to destroy the venom. Various methods have been employed, including a hot iron, burning gunpowder and caustic chemical agents. For obvious reasons, this type of treatment is very painful and destructive of flesh around the snakebite. Cauterization of a snakebite has not been shown to confer any clinical benefit.[82]

MASSAGING THE SNAKEBITE

It is tempting in the moment to massage or manipulate the location of the snakebite to encourage it to bleed in hopes of eliminating some of the venom. This practice may result in forcing the venom further into the interstitial spaces in the flesh where it is collected by the *lymphatics* and should not be attempted.[83]

Along the same lines, a study on human volunteers showed that blood from a mimicked snake fang wound contained a very small amount of the injected mock venom.[84]

EVACUATING THE VICTIM

Once you have treated the victim to the extent possible, it is of paramount importance to get him to a hospital as soon as possible whether or not you see signs of envenomation.

Always ask for help. Don't be shy about asking passers-by for help in dealing with the snakebite or in evacuating the victim.

Making the decision whether to evacuate the victim or wait for rescue is complicated by many factors and should be approached calmly and deliberately by discussion with the victim and those around him. This can be a challenging decision and may include such factors as:

- The distance to the trailhead
- The terrain

- The weather
- The time of day
- The size of the victim
- The age of the victim
- The resources at hand, human and otherwise
- The availability of a rescue service
- The availability of a communication link with a rescue service, e.g., cellphone or shortwave radio

You have essentially **three choices** regarding the evacuation decision:
- No evacuation. Immobilize the victim and wait for the rescue service to arrive.
- Walk or carry the victim all the way to the trailhead.
- Walk or carry the victim until you meet up with the rescue service, which would then carry the victim the rest of the way.

The latter two are appropriate when the victim can immobilize the afflicted extremity so that muscular contraction does not increase lymphatic flow while walking. He should proceed slowly toward the trailhead, being careful not to increase his heart rate over what it already is as a result of the snakebite.

The latter two are also appropriate when there is some overriding reason to move the victim before rescue arrives, such as impending flood, wildfire, severe weather, lack of adequate resources to endure bad weather or stay overnight, and so on.

Specifically,

- If the victim is alone, not within cellphone range, and not likely to be encountered by any others (for example, the typical solo hunter), he has no choice but to **walk out slowly** while trying to keep his heart rate and respiration as slow as possible. He should first apply a pressure bandage. If the bite is in an upper extremity, he should sling it before proceeding.

- If the snakebite is in a leg, he should, if possible, cut two saplings to use as crutches so that he does not have to walk on the afflicted leg. Having a drywall saw, camp saw, or hunting knife with serrated edges would greatly facilitate making crutches and should be standard equipment. Calls for help should continue.

- If the victim is with others, they can assist him by carrying his pack and by **helping him to walk** by putting the victim's arms around their shoulders. If the snakebite is in the lower extremity, that extremity should be immobilized and not used for walking. The muscular action of walking increases the lymph flow in the extremity and could lead to earlier systemic effects. Again, **get help from others on the trail**!

- If the bite is on an upper extremity, it should be immobilized with a sling, and then walk the victim toward the trailhead, being careful to keep the heartbeat and respirations down.

- Continue to **talk to the victim** to keep him calm and assess his condition. If you have not already reached rescue services on your cellphone, stop and try to call periodically.

- If sufficient resources are available, the best evacuation choice would be to make a stretcher using field expedients available at the site and carry the victim out. Once more, **always ask for help**!

- In all cases, continue trying to call for help, or if you have sufficient resources, send ahead for help.

SNAKEBITE VACCINE AND IMMUNIZATION

Immunization from snakebite effects for humans (also called venom desensitization therapy) has not been well established at this date.[85]

There is anecdotal evidence that repeated injections of snakebite venom in humans can result in immunization of the injected individual. Bill Haast, an amateur herpetologist in Florida owned thousands of snakes. He began injecting himself with diluted amounts of snake venom in 1948 and gradually increased the amounts. He developed an immunity to snakebites and was bitten over 170 times, none of which was the cause of his death at age100.[86]

However, a review of the medical literature reveals no scientifically controlled experiments to immunize humans from the effects of any or all snakebite venom.

Hedgehogs, mongooses, honey badgers and a few birds that feed on snakes are known to be immune to snake venom.[87]

DOGS

Dogs are particularly susceptible to snakebite because they are more likely to encounter a snake if they are unleashed and range back and forth around the trail. The response and treatment for dogs is the same as for humans. If possible, the dog should be carried to the trailhead. You can rig a hammock for the dog with a jacket or pack, which two or three people can carry.

There is a snakebite vaccine for dogs.[88] Contact your vet to discuss its availability and efficacy against snakes in your location. There is also anti-venom for dogs.

There are also classes to teach your dog how to avoid a rattlesnake bite. A trained dog may alert you to the presence of a rattlesnake that you don't see.

HORSES

Snakebites of horses are seldom fatal except where the horse's nostrils swell shut. Horses can't breathe through their mouth, so they will basically suffocate if their nostrils are occluded. To avoid this insert a piece of a garden hose or a trimmed syringe into each nostril so they remain open as the face swells. Tape the ends of the hose or syringe to soften the ends. Once the nose swells, the pressure will hold it in place.

Once you have taken care of the immediate breathing problem, call your vet or take the horse to the vet. In the meantime, keep the horse quiet. Remove the horse's bridle so it won't cut into the skin if the face swells. If you are a long way from home or your trailer, get off and walk slowly to the nearest place you can get professional help.

Holding a horse's head up when you encounter a snake may keep it from getting bitten on the nose—or maybe for the second time.[89]

SNAKE REPELLANTS

Various snake repellants are available on the commercial market. Unfortunately, none of them has proven effective. The same holds true for mothballs, sulfur, gourd vines, cedar oil, and king snake musk.[90]

INCIDENT REPORT FORM

In all emergency medical situations, it is important to keep track of the victim's signs and symptoms, vital signs, and care rendered, as well as personal information, such as name, address, someone to notify, and so on. The best way to do this is either on your cell phone or by using an incident report form. An example is provided as Appendix A. Hand off the information to the rescuers or ambulance attendants when they arrive.

— CHAPTER 2 —

ACUTE MOUNTAIN ILLNESS

In May 1966 eight climbers, some of them extremely experienced, died on Mt. Everest in the middle of a raging storm. Although many on the mountain that day managed to make it to safety, the storm, and the accompanying cold and wind, made travel difficult. And they were in the "death zone," that place on high mountains where the air is so thin that there's not enough oxygen to support life for long. According to author Jon Krakauer, after he ran out of oxygen near the top of Everest, "I felt like I was suffocating. My vision dimmed and my head began to spin. I was on the brink of losing consciousness." [91] He and the others on the mountain that day, including the ones who died, were suffering from *acute mountain illness*. Ask anyone who's been there. Acute mountain illness is not fun. You feel just terrible, and it could get worse, even deadly. So, what exactly is AMI?

TYPES OF ACUTE MOUNTAIN ILLNESSES

Acute mountain illness (AMI) is generally described as a galaxy of **physiological and psychological symptoms** which are often experienced from ascending too rapidly in the mountains, although it can occur anywhere the requisite conditions are met, such as someone flying from New York City which is at sea level to Mexico City at 7,350 feet 2,240 meters).

AMI typically includes:
- Acute mountain sickness (AMS)
- High altitude cerebral edema (HACE)
- High altitude pulmonary edema (HAPE)[92]

Other altitude-related pathologies are:
- High altitude retinal hemorrhage (HARH)
- Altitude-induced peripheral edema (AIPE).
- High altitude flatus expulsion
- High altitude pharyngitis/bronchitis (HAPB)
- Sleep Apnea

THOSE AT RISK FOR ACUTE MOUNTAIN ILLNESS

There are numerous population groups which are susceptible to AMI, including anyone who might be at an altitude with a *hypoxic* (low oxygen) *environment* to which they are unaccustomed, including:

- Joggers and runners
- Hikers and trekkers
- Mountain bikers and road bikers
- Climbers
- Backpackers
- Downhill and cross-country skiers
- Hunters and anglers
- Aviators and passengers in unpressurized airplanes
- Hang gliders

- Paragliders
- Base jumpers
- Skydivers
- Tourists driving over mountain passes
- Tourists traveling to higher altitudes such as Machu Picchu (8189 feet; 2430 meters)
- Tourists riding cable cars to mountain tops
- Mountain hut hosts and guests
- Workers in mountain concessions
- Mountain highway construction and maintenance workers
- Mountain highway snowplow drivers
- Rangers and law enforcement officers
- Wildfire fighters
- Emergency medical services personnel
- Mountain rescue services
- Soldiers on foot
- Airborne soldiers
- Porters for mountain expeditions
- Mountain guides
- Pilgrims to mountain religious shrines
- Astronomers at observatories
- Miners (the former mining community of Leadville, Colorado is at 10,000 feet, or 3,048 meters)
- Birdwatchers
- Professional and amateur nature photographers
- Residents returning to altitude who have lost their acclimatization

ACUTE MOUNTAIN ILLNESS IN GENERAL

AMI is caused primarily by *hypoxia*, that is, an **insufficient supply of oxygen** delivered to the body's tissues by the red blood cells. Hypoxia, in turn, is caused primarily by **decreased barometric pressure** in the air as you ascend to a higher altitude (*hypobaric hypoxia*). Although the percent of oxygen in the air remains constant at 20.9

percent at all elevations, the amount of oxygen delivered to the tissues in real terms declines proportionately with increases in elevation. At some point, as one ascends, the amount of oxygen in the blood falls to a level at which symptoms of AMI are triggered, and there are measurable changes in the body's responses, both physical and cognitive. Hypoxia will immediately **impair maximal and prolonged whole-body physical performance capabilities** by amounts generally proportional to the elevation.

Unfortunately, the link between hypoxia and AMI isn't clear. Current thinking is that hypoxia causes the blood vessels of the brain to dilate in an attempt to get more oxygen. Something about this vasodilation causes a headache. And because there is more blood in the brain, the brain is slightly swollen. Although everyone going to high altitude has slight brain swelling, it is worse in those who develop AMI. As swelling increases, so does pressure on the brain, and this might be the cause of the symptoms.[93]

"Higher level brain functions involving cognition, decision-making, and reasoning are most sensitive to the effects of altitude and oxygen deprivation."[94]

Hypoxia becomes apparent and medically significant around 1200 meters (3,937 feet).[95]

TECHNO-SPEAK: More specifically, because the barometric pressure of inspired oxygen (PiO2) decreases as you ascend, there is a drop in the pressure of inspired oxygen in the *alveoli* (PAO2), the tiny, balloon-like structures in the lungs which expand and contract as we breathe. This results in a drop in arterial pressure of oxygen (PaO2) in the blood, a drop in arterial oxygen saturation (SaO2) and finally, reduced oxygen delivered to the tissues.[96]

ACUTE MOUNTAIN SICKNESS (AMS)

SYMPTOMS OF ACUTE MOUNTAIN SICKNESS

The most benign manifestation of AMI is acute mountain sickness (**AMS**). AMS is a clinical diagnosis based on some or all the following typical symptoms while ascending to higher altitudes:

- Headache
- Fatigue

- Poor appetite
- Nausea or vomiting
- Light-headedness
- Sleep disturbances
- Feeling chilled
- Sometimes irritability[97]

Victims often describe altitude sickness as "feeling just awful."

These symptoms are often mistaken for, and diagnosed as, other pathologies, like the flu, alcohol hangover, exhaustion, migraine, hypothermia, CO poisoning, pneumonia, asthma, congestive heart failure, heart attack, pulmonary embolus, and/or dehydration.[98]

No blood work or other tests are necessary to diagnose AMS, except to rule out other possible diagnoses. Symptoms may take days to develop or may occur within hours, depending on the rate of ascent and the altitude attained.[99]

For the most part victims of AMS will **adjust to the current altitude** in a period of twelve hours to several days, and therefore may stay at the same altitude if symptoms aren't too bad.[100] In other words, wait it out, and maybe it will get better.

PULSE OXIMETRY (OXYGEN SATURATION LEVEL IN THE BLOOD)

Pulse oximetry is a noninvasive and painless test that measures your *oxygen saturation level,* (SaO2), that is, the **oxygen levels in your blood**. Knowing your SaO2 is often helpful in diagnosing AMS when a person feels bad and there is no other obvious explanation. On the other hand, a normal pulse oximetry reading would indicate there is some other reason the individual feels bad, and your triage should continue.

Remember to **continue with your triage** even if you find an abnormally low pulse oximetry level. There may be other causes present, such as heart disease, diabetes, or drug overdose.

Pulse oximetry is measured using a *pulse oximeter*, a small, clip-like device familiar to most of us, which fits over an earlobe or the end of a finger or toe. [101] The normal acceptable range of oxygen saturation in the blood is between 90 percent and 100 percent. You can expect this figure to be lower at higher altitudes until you become acclimatized. Pulse oximeters will also typically indicate a person's pulse rate.

Notwithstanding their usefulness, note that the **readings may not be accurate** due to a cold finger, toe, or earlobe (which will cause under-reporting), moving around, talking, stimulation, *voluntary hyperventilation* (rapid breathing), recent ingestion of food or caffeinated beverages or exercise (which will cause over-reporting).[102] Also, a pulse oximeter will not work if the individual has fingernail or toenail polish.

Reynaud's syndrome, a congenital condition resulting in poor circulation to the hands and feet, may make it difficult to obtain a reading on the pulse oximeter.[103] The best practice is to test each individual's response to the pulse oximeter before the climb to identify any abnormalities.

Pulse oximeters are very light and should be a component of every mountaineer's first aid kit. They can be purchased online for $10 to $50 online. Their batteries need to be replaced periodically.

Pulse Oximetry Levels and The Expected Incidence Of AMS at Different Altitudes:

✓ **"Low"** altitude
Under 3,937 feet (1,200 meters) - No altitude effects

✓ **"Moderate"** altitude
3,937 to 7,856 feet (1,200 to 2400m) – Pulse ox: above 92%; Expected incidence of AMS: 0%-20%
Acclimatization begins.

✓ **"High"** altitude
7,856 to 13,093 feet (2,400 to 4,000m) – Pulse ox: 80% - 92%; Expected incidence of AMS: 20% - 80%
Work performance progressively impaired'

✓ **"Very High"** altitude
13,093 to 18,003 feet (4,000 to 5,500m) – Pulse ox: 70% - 80%; Expected incidence of AMS: > 80%
Profound impairments of physical and cognitive abilities; it begins to get worse faster.

✓ **"Extremely High"** altitude

Greater than 18,003 feet (5,500m) – Pulse ox: < 60% to 70%: Expected incidence of AMS: 100%

High probability of developing fatal altitude illness.[104]

Also, there are several questionnaire-based diagnostic tools which can be useful to diagnose AMS, such as the Lake Louise Scoring System.

THE LAKE LOUISE SCORING SYSTEM

Another way of evaluating a person for AMI is the Lake Louise Scoring System. In 1991, a committee of experts at a conference in Lake Louise, Canada proposed a scoring system for assessing the severity of symptoms, known as the **Lake Louise acute mountain sickness scoring system**. The system was modified in 2018. An individual has acute mountain sickness if they fulfill the following criteria: (a) recent ascent in altitude, (b) headache, and a total symptom score of 3 or more.[105]

Symptom	Score
Headache:	
None at all	0
A mild headache	1
Moderate headache	2
Severe headache, incapacitating	3
Gastrointestinal symptoms:	
Good appetite	0
Poor appetite or nausea	1
Moderate nausea or vomiting	2
Severe nausea and vomiting, incapacitating	**3**
Fatigue and/or weakness:	
Not tired or weak	0
Mild fatigue/weakness	1

Moderate fatigue/weakness	2
Severe fatigue/weakness, incapacitating	3

Dizzy/light-headed:

Not dizziness/light-headedness	0
Mild dizziness/light-headedness	1
Moderate dizziness/light-headedness	2
Severe dizziness/light-headedness	3
Incapacitating	

AMS Clinical Functional Score

Overall, if you had AMS symptoms, how did they affect your activities?

0 – Not at all
1 – Symptoms present but did not force any change in activity or itinerary.
2 – My symptoms forced me to stop the ascent or to go down on my own power.
3 – Had to be evacuated to a lower level.

ONSET OF ACUTE MOUNTAIN SICKNESS

AMS can arise at different times. Sometimes it is apparent soon after arrival at altitude. At other times its onset may be delayed for several hours or more. AMS typically doesn't develop after a couple of days of feeling well. If a person doing fine feels sick after two or three days, you need to suspect other causes for her illness.[106] For those doing long day hikes at altitude, AMS might appear before the hike is half over.

THE BODY'S PHYSIOLOGICAL RESPONSE TO ACUTE MOUNTAIN SICKNESS

At first your body responds to increases in altitude by escalating the **rate and depth of your breathing** and **your pulse rate** to deliver more oxygen to the cells and remove more waste products. Also **changes in kidney function** cause the blood to become more alkaline, which allows it to take up and deliver more oxygen to the tissues.[107]

LATER ADAPTATIONS

After a couple of weeks your body begins to make more red blood cells, a process which that enhances your ability to take up and utilize oxygen.[108]

ACUTE MOUNTAIN SICKNESS DURING PREGNANCY

AMS incidence is not different during pregnancy.[109]

HIGH ALTITUDE CEREBRAL EDEMA

High altitude cerebral edema (HACE) is a potentially fatal accumulation of fluid in brain tissue.[110] It is essentially caused by leaky blood vessels that cause swelling of the brain,[111] and is thought to be a progression of the cerebral effects of AMS.

SYMPTOMS OF HIGH-ALTITUDE CEREBRAL EDEMA

Typically, HACE is characterized by a **change in the mental status** of the individual (for example, confusion, disorientation, inability to talk coherently), *truncal ataxia*, (swaying of the upper body when walking), severe headache, nausea, vomiting and extreme lassitude. There can also be other neurologically related changes such as visual abnormalities, numb or tingling parts of the body, bowel and bladder malfunction, hallucinations (visual or auditory) and seizures. Rapid pulse, cyanosis and general pallor are commonly present[112] Decreased consciousness which can lead to coma and death is the inevitable outcome if left untreated.[113]

AMS and HACE are considered a spectrum of the same altitude illness. HACE usually occurs t altitudes over 13,000 feet (3,963 meters).[114] If you have previously had HACE, there is a high likelihood you will have it again.[115]

A standard test for HACE is to see if the individual can walk a straight line, heel to toe, without displaying *truncal ataxia*, that is, losing balance or missing a step.

Care should be taken to not confuse HACE with other possible pathologies such as *stroke, transient ischemic attack (TIA)*, infection, trauma, dehydration, *hypoglycemia*, and substance abuse.

HIGH ALTITUDE PULMONARY EDEMA

High altitude pulmonary edema (HAPE) is **excess fluid in the lungs** with the result that the individual cannot get enough oxygen.

SYMPTOMS OF HIGH-ALTITUDE PULMONARY EDEMA

Mt. Everest is in the "Death Zone"

Symptoms include difficult or labored breathing, especially while at rest (*dyspnea*), rapid heart rate (*tachycardia*), a bluish hue to the skin, gums, fingernails, or mucous membranes caused by a lack of oxygen (*cyanosis*), frothy, pink-tinted sputum (colored by blood leaking into the lungs), and crackles/wheezing in the lungs. As a result of these symptoms, HAPE is often misdiagnosed or mistreated as pneumonia.[116] The individual may also be drowsy and may become extremely agitated, disoriented and sweaty. Confusion, collapse, coma, and ultimately death will follow if left untreated.[117]

TECHNO-SPEAK: With HAPE the blood pressure in the lungs rises in response to low oxygen levels. In some areas of the lungs, the blood vessels cannot contain high pressure and breakdown of the small vessels causes leaking of fluid cross the membranes into the air sacs. Hence the pink-tinted sputum. [118]

HAPE is not necessarily preceded by AMS.

RE-ENTRY HAPE

Re-entry HAPE happens when people who live at high altitude go to a lower altitude for a few days and get HAPE when they return.[119]

HIGH ALTITUDE RETINAL HEMORRHAGE (HARH)

HARH refers to small hemorrhages that occur at the back of the eye on the retina at altitude. Development near the macula causes blurring of vision, loss of central vision or dark spots,[120] otherwise, it is symptomless and self-limiting.[121] It typically resolves itself within ten to fourteen days. People going to altitude for the first time are more susceptible to retinal hemorrhages than experienced climbers and high-altitude dwellers.[122] *Hypoxia*, that is, insufficient oxygen in the eye, is thought to be the cause. Although a benign condition, it may be a warning of other, more serious manifestations of AMI. [123]

The remedy for HARH is to refrain from further strenuous activities which might increase blood pressure in the eye, and to descend. [124]

ALTITUDE-INDUCED PERIPHERAL EDEMA (AIPE)

AIPE refers to *edema* or swelling of the face or extremities. It is relatively common and is not considered cause for descent in the absence of other symptoms of AMS. AIPE is more common in women than men, although it is not related to the menstrual cycle or oral contraceptives. It is often found in individuals with other altitude illnesses.

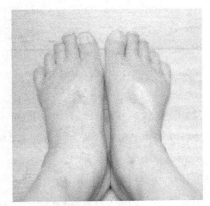

Peripheral Edema

Differential (alternative) diagnoses of AIPE include congestive heart failure, cirrhosis, renal failure, allergic reactions and edema of the upper extremities caused by pack straps (so-called **pack strap edema**.)

Descent is not required, but it is the choice of treatment.[125]

HIGH ALTITUDE PHARYNGITIS/BRONCHITIS (HAPB)

HAPB is an irritation of the mucosal lining of the respiratory passage. It is caused by breathing cold, dry air at altitude. Signs and symptoms are sore throat, chronic cough, and severe cough spasms which sometimes cause rib fractures. Hydration, and a breathable balaclava can help to minimize respiratory heat and moisture loss.[126]

HIGH ALTITUDE FLATUS EXPULSION (HAFE)

HAFE occurs because gases trapped in your intestine expand at the lower pressures, which are found at altitude. The increased volume of gas is released by farting.[127] Although a source of embarrassment, it is of no medical concern. Avoiding foods known to cause flatulence, such as beans, is often helpful. Beano tablets may also serve to reduce flatulence.

PERIODIC BREATHING—SLEEP APNEA

Interruptions to sleep at altitude caused by reduced oxygen in the blood (*hypoxia*) are referred to as **sleep apnea**, or periodic breathing. Sleep quality is disturbed which prevents revitalizing rest and impairs daytime performance. Impairment decreases when oxygen saturation increases with acclimatization.

TECHNO-SPEAK: Periodic breathing results from the conflict between the body's oxygen sensors and its CO_2 sensors: "Oxygen sensors in the body tell the brain to increase breathing, which causes the lungs to blow off CO_2. But then CO_2 sensors tell the brain to stop breathing because CO_2 stores are getting too low. The result is that breathing stops for a few seconds until the oxygen sensors tell it to start again. It is treated by taking acetazolamide (Diamox) before bedtime."[128] Check out the side effects and try it at home first.

HIGH ALTITUDE SYNCOPE

Occasionally, travelers to moderate altitude will experience a brief fainting episode during the first 24 hours. This generally has to do with changes in blood pressure that occur at altitude. These episodes are not serious and are not associated with AMI.[129]

TREATMENT OF ACUTE MOUNTAIN ILLNESS

AMI can be treated, but keep in mind, **unexplained symptoms** after altitude gain should be treated as acute mountain sickness until proven otherwise.

Remain in place. AMS usually resolves itself within 6 to 48 hours, so remaining in place may be the answer to your AMI. Do NOT proceed to a higher altitude if you have AMI.

Retreating to a lower altitude is by far the preferred remedy for AMI.[130] If the symptoms are mild, returning to a previous asymptomatic altitude is reasonable. If the symptoms continue to worsen or are severe, descending 1640 feet (500 meters) is advised.[131] Considering the serious consequences if not treated, in cases of HACE and HAPE the victim should be taken to a lower altitude and transported to a location where definitive medical treatment is available.

If enough rescuers are available, it would be helpful to carry a severely affected victim and thus reduce his need for oxygen from the exertion of down-climbing.

Headache is often the presenting symptom of AMS.[132] **Brain swelling** induced by hypoxia is the most likely culprit. Other risk factors are low hydration, overexertion and insufficient energy intake. As in the case of other types of headache, taking aspirin if you are not allergic to it, Tylenol (acetaminophen), or ibuprofen is appropriate with adequate rest and hydration.[133] Anti-emetics can be taken for **nausea.**

Since *hypoxia*, that is, **low oxygen content in the blood**, is at the root of all AMI, it makes sense to treat the victim with oxygen, if it is available. Oxygen is administered from an oxygen tank through a nasal cannula, initially at the rate of 0.5 – 2 LPM (liters per minute) for AMS. HACE and HAPE will require much higher rates of oxygen, in severe cases as much as 15 LPM administered through a mask.[134] Many ski resorts now offer oxygen bars or even separate units to take to your room. Although anecdotal reports state that some relief is felt, doctors warn that such benefits are short-lived, may be merely a placebo effect, and will continue only as long as you are using the oxygen.[135]

Oxygen is particularly effective if used while **sleeping**, the time when it is most needed. It is also administered at the rate of 0.5 – 2 LPM. During waking hours we tend to breathe faster and deeper to make up for low oxygen intake without even realizing it. But when we go to sleep, we breathe as though we are at a lower altitude, so oxygen levels fall. The solution, if available, is to hook up to oxygen while sleeping.[136] High altitude headache will usually resolve after a few minutes of supplemental oxygen [137]

Canned oxygen is relatively new on the scene. Users claim to experience a positive effect, but doctors point out that it is temporary, and oxygen will help you only as long as you are using it. There has been no scientific research that this extra shot of pure oxygen has any benefits. Healthy individuals take in approximately 21 percent oxygen from the air they breathe. At that level, blood is almost completely (99 percent) saturated, meaning there is no need for additional oxygen.[138]

The best advice is to buy a can and then go to a higher altitude and check your pulse oximetry while breathing the ambient air there. Then take a few breaths from your canned oxygen and recheck your pulse oximetry. If the oxygen is effective, there should be an increase in your pulse oximetry reading. But then check your pulse oximetry reading again later after breathing ambient air for a few minutes to see if you are getting any lasting effect.

Some users have reported testing cans of oxygen and found there was little or no oxygen.

Keep in mind too that the directions on how to use canned oxygen can require you to inspire some ambient air along with the canned oxygen, thus diluting its effect. Also, if you share a can, you run the risk of sharing harmful bacteria as well.

Anecdotal evidence of the beneficial effects of oxygen, at least short term, is available at every home game of the Denver Broncos played in the Mile High City when opposing players are seen donning oxygen masks after coming off the playing field.

More extensive remedies. Where professional rescue is available or where more extensively organized mountaineering expeditions are planned, a Gamow bag, an oxygen concentrator, a Continuous Positive Air Pressure device (CPAP) and certain prescription drugs might be available.

GAMOW BAGS

The Gamow Hyperbaric Bag was invented by Dr. Igor Gamow of the University of Colorado in Boulder and carries Food and Drug Administration approval for the treatment of

Inflated Gamow Bag

acute altitude illness. It is **a portable, air-tight, cylindrical bag** of coated nylon which is big enough for a person to lie down in. Air is pumped into the Gamow Bag with a hand pump, foot pump, or air compressor to a pressure of 2 psi. Bleed-off valves release air once the pressure in the bag reaches 2 psi. An attached manometer ensures that the valves are functioning properly and pressure is maintained. The Gamow bag weights about 3.2k. It appears that mild cases of altitude illness respond relatively quickly to Gamow bag treatment, while more severe cases may require extended treatment periods. This may represent a limitation of use, since pumping for extended periods of time at high altitude is quite exhausting, unless several rescuers are available.

Be aware that victims may feel extremely claustrophobic and panicky in a Gamow bag. Continuous presence and reassurance of a rescuer can help to alleviate these feelings. The rescuer should be positioned so the victim can see her through the window at all times. Showing the victim how to extricate himself from the Gamow bag also helps reduce his anxiety.

A portable, battery or solar powered **oxygen concentrator** may provide as much as 3 liters per minute of oxygen. Another helpful device, a **CPAP,** is designed to force air into the victim's lungs at low pressure through a mask worn over the nose and mouth or using a nasal cannula. It has been analogized to hanging your head outside of the window of a moving vehicle, facing into the wind. When a CPAP is employed, arterial oxygen saturations increase and symptoms of AMS decrease.[139]

ACETAZOLAMIDE (DIAMOX)

Acetazolamide (Diamox) is a drug which has proven to be useful in stimulating breathing and diminishing sleep disorders associated with AMS which facilitates the body's normal adjustment to high altitude[140] and reduces symptoms of AMS.[141] Although acetazolamide is not available without a prescription, it would make sense to carry a supply and be familiar with its administration when attempting ultra-high peaks.

TECHNO-SPEAK: Acetazolamide forces the kidneys to excrete bicarbonate. "Increasing the amount of bicarbonate excreted in the urine causes the blood to become more acidic. The body equates acidity of the blood to its CO_2 concentration, and artificially acidifying the blood fools the body into thinking it has an excess of CO_2. It eliminates this perceived excess CO_2 by deeper and faster breathing, which in turn increases the amount of oxygen in the blood."[142]

The use of acetazolamide is contra-indicated **during pregnancy** because of' the risk of *teratogenicity*, or abnormal growth of the fetus.[143]

DEXAMETHASONE AND NIFEDIPINE

Dexamethasone and **nifedipine** also can improve the symptoms of acute mountain sickness, as can **tadalafil** and **sildenafil**. These drugs are not available without a prescription from your medical provider.

It would be a good idea to test these drugs at home before the climb to see if they have any adverse other side effects, such as *paresthesia* ("pins and needles" sensation, often occurring in the arms, legs, hands and feet), *polyuria* (increased urination) and depression.[144] Also, be sure to check out the side effects of all these drugs before using them.

Ibuprofen taken 6 hours before climbing to high elevations and then taking it every 6 hours while climbing may help prevent altitude sickness.[145]

PREVENTION OF ACUTE MOUNTAIN ILLNESS

ACCLIMATIZATION

Acclimatization is the best form of prevention of AMI. Acclimatization refers to the body's physiological adaptations that develop during continuous or intermittent exposure to hypoxia.[146] There is abundant evidence, both clinical and anecdotal, that **a slow, measured ascent** allows the body to acclimatize and reduces the risk of developing AMI. Generally, safe acclimatization above 3000m (9840 feet) is to limit daily altitude gain to 300m (984 feet) with a rest day for every 1,000m (3,281 feet) of altitude gain.[147] Keep in mind that the appropriate rate of ascent is different for everyone, so don't allow yourself to get pushed past your limit by the faster hikers in your group.

Once acclimatization at a given altitude is achieved, it will be retained as long as the altitude exposure continues.[148] Acclimatization can be lost after only a few days at low altitude, and a person may again incur AMS.[149] **De-acclimatization** or loss of acclimatization occurs at approximately the same rate or faster than acclimatization develops.[150]

Climbers should sleep at the lowest altitude that does not interfere with the purpose of the climb. The usual mantra is, **"Climb high, sleep low."**[151]

When available, the periodic use of a **hypobaric chamber** or similar device to simulate altitude gains before actually climbing can provide **intermittent altitude (hypoxic) exposure (IHE)**. The hypobaric chamber reduces the atmospheric pressure and the amount of oxygen available to the user to stimulate the body's normal reaction to AMS and thus lead to acclimatization. **Normobaric hypoxic devices** are nitrogen dilution systems which dilute ambient air with nitrogen to produce hypoxic air, that is, air with less than 20.9 percent oxygen which is then delivered to the user through a mask, hood, tent or room.[152]

DRUG THERAPY

Acetazolamide (Diamox) is also effective in speeding up acclimatization. The drug is typically started the night before the planned ascent and continued until descent is initiated or until the individual has been at the target elevation for two or three days. You should familiarize yourself with the side effects of Diamox before taking it. Dexamethasone can be used as a substitute by those who can't take acetazolamide.[153]

HYDRATION

Hydration is important in avoiding AMS. With each breath we blow off a certain amount of moisture from our lungs. The effect is amplified at altitude where the air is drier. Accordingly, it is important to stay hydrated. Regular and sufficient fluid intake inhibits *hypohydration* (dehydration) and helps to prevent AMS.

CARBO-LOADING

In a hypoxic environment, **carbohydrates** are the most efficient energy source, that is, they provide the most *adenosine triphosphate (ATP),* per molecule of oxygen inhaled.[154] Since AMS is caused by a lack of sufficient oxygen, eating a carbohydrate-rich diet, will leave more oxygen available to fight off AMS. There is some limited clinical evidence that a high carbohydrate diet is a way to prevent AMS. [155]

Peak-bagging is common among hikers in Colorado where I live. For most that can mean going from mile-high Denver (5280 feet, 1609 meters), or some similar altitude, to the top of a fourteen-thousand-foot mountain in a single day, an increase of 8,000 feet (2,439 meters) or more. A cheap way to prepare for these challenges is to drive up to a higher elevation several times in the days preceding the attempt on the peak and spend a few hours there. One can actually go on a paved road to the top of Mt. Evans outside of Denver, which tops out at 14,265 feet (4,349 meters). There's a herd of friendly mountain goats there which is always fun to see, and with lunch and a book it's easy to just chill for a few hours while you are acclimatizing. The views are spectacular in all directions.

CAFFEINE

Contrary to conventional wisdom, **caffeine** use at high altitude is not only safe, but beneficial in that it helps to release energy. However there is no evidence that ingestion of coffee or tea will forestall the onset of AMS. Nor is there any evidence that the diuresis which occurs from drinking coffee or tea is substantial enough to warrant not drinking caffeinated beverages. **Habitual coffee and tea drinkers** should not stop drinking because the symptoms of caffeine withdrawal are similar to AMS.[156]

SLEEPING AIDS

If you are not sleeping well because of periodic breathing, Diamox (acet-azolamide) should be the first choice of medication to improve sleep. Benzodiaz-epines such as temazepam (Restoril) lorazepam (Ativan), diazepam (Valium) and alprazolam (Xanax) should generally be avoided as they decrease the breathing drive, especially when combined with alcohol. Sleep medications such as zolpidem (Ambien) andeszopicone, (Lunesta) are safe at altitude and seem to work well with-out affecting the breathing drive. Some people use over-the-counter sleep aids such as Tylenol PM which contains Benadryl, an antihistamine. Antihistamines have not been shown to affect breathing and may be taken safely. The sleeping aide, Trazadone, does not decrease your breathing and is safe to take at altitude. [157]

GINKO BILOBA

There is conflicting evidence as to the effectiveness of gingko biloba in the pre-vention of acute mountain sickness.[158] There are not enough clinical data to show conclusively whether gingko biloba can prevent AMS or not [159]

ALCOHOL

Alcohol suppresses breathing and can result in lower blood oxygen, and thus should be avoided while at altitude. [160]

SMOKING

Results of research regarding the effects of smoking on AMS have been quite variable. Some say that smoking may represent some sort of **acclimatization to hypoxia** and is associated with a slight decrease in the risk of AMS.[161] Others say smoking is a distinct risk factor for AMS for workers employed at high altitudes and should be avoided.[162] Another research team found that smoking slightly decreases the risk of AMS, but impairs long-term altitude acclimatization and lung function during a prolonged stay at high altitude.[163]

PHYSICAL FITNESS

It doesn't help to avoid AMS by being physically fit. Younger people think they can push through the effects of AMS because they are fit and healthy, but there is no science to support this position.

SIDE EFFECTS OF ACCLIMATIZATION

Altitude acclimatization has **no negative side effects** and will not affect your health or physical performance when you return to low altitude. [164]

PRE-EXISTING MEDICAL CONDITIONS

People with **asthma**, surprisingly enough, do better at altitude, probably because of the absence of pollution and dust mites.

Any pre-existing condition which interferes with oxygenation of the body is likely to add to the risk of AMI. Thus, **COPD sufferers** do worse at altitude.

A comprehensive discussion of pre-existing conditions is beyond the scope of this chapter. Good summaries may be found in the medical literature.[165] Persons with pre-existing conditions should consult with their doctor before going to altitude.

PREDISPOSITION TO AMI - INDIVIDUAL SUSCEPTIBILITY

The likelihood of AMS depends in part on an individual's susceptibility. Studies have shown that some individuals are more prone to HAPE than others. An individual's past performance at altitude is the main predictor of his future performance.

OBESITY

There is a some evidence that obese individuals are more likely to develop AMS at altitude than non-obese individuals For example, obesity reduces the *ventilator response* (increased breathing as a result of being at altitude), resulting in *oxygen desaturation* (reduced oxygen in the system) and *periodic apneic breathing* (intermittent breathing). As a result, there is less oxygen in the blood, which **predisposes obese people** to AMS. It isn't clear whether obesity is a high-risk factor for developing HAPE.[166]

PREGNANCY

Being pregnant will **not increase the risk of AMI** at moderate altitudes. In fact, the increased *progesterone* of pregnancy causes the woman to breathe more at altitude than non-pregnant women which keeps their oxygen level higher, and helps to prevent AMI.[167] Travel to moderate altitudes, around 8,000 feet (2,439 meters) should not be a problem for pregnant women.[168] The decision to travel to high altitude should be tempered by the knowledge that in the event of problems in the pregnancy, the mother may be a long way from medical help.

EFFECTS OF GENDER ON AMI

Susceptibility to AMS is not different between males and females.[169] A woman's **menstrual cycle** has no effect on ventilator acclimatization, blood oxygenation, cardiac output, glucose utilization, or exercise performance.[170]

CHILDREN

Children get AMI just as adults do, and just as often. Unfortunately, children, particularly young children, are not very good at communicating their symptoms, and therefore **their illness is underdiagnosed.** Fussiness, irritability, increased crying, and food refusal may indicate AMI in children. [171]

OLDER PEOPLE

Older people suffer from AMS no more often than their younger counterparts. On the contrary, despite the increased prevalence of pre-existing medical conditions with age, the risk of AMS has been found to be lower in older people.[172] There is some evidence that this is because of the decrease in brain size with advancing years.[173]

LONG-TERM SEQUELAE FROM HIGH ALTITUDE EXPOSURE

A study of 35 climbers ascending Mt. Everest, and other high peaks concluded that high-altitude climbing carries a risk of developing **cerebral lesions and atrophy**, and that the risk is higher in non-properly acclimatized subjects.[174]

In other words, on really high climbs you are going to lose some brain cells.

— CHAPTER 3 —

LIGHTNING

It was a typical June day in the Colorado mountains—so of course, it rained and snowed and sleeted on us all afternoon. We were in Rocky Mountain National Park, north of Denver. Our plan was to climb the First Buttress on Hallet Peak, and we weren't going to let a little bad weather stop us. So up we went. A thousand feet of technical climbing. We both slipped and fell twice, but the rope caught us, and finally, late in the evening, we were on top!

We had made it! **We beat the mountain!** We beat the weather, and then

FLASH! BOOM!

Lightning hit my partner in the head, melted the frame on his pack and blew his shoe off! I was about twenty feet away and felt nothing. I looked over at him as if to say, "Boy, that was a close one," and I saw him lying there, steam rising off his body.

I ran over. "Glenn, Glenn," I shouted. His eyes were wide open, pupils completely dilated. I started CPR. Chest compressions. Rescue breaths. Chest compressions. Rescue breaths. Over and over, but nothing was working. I was frantic! I slapped his chest like we used to in the old days in hopes it would start his heart. Nothing! I could see in the waning light that he was getting cyanotic; his skin was taking on a bluish tint. More compressions! More rescue breaths! I went on and on until I was exhausted, and then I realized: **He was dead.**

By then it was almost ten o'clock, and that's when things started getting really weird. Suddenly, it felt like something out there was going to come back and get me. Some **yellow-eyed beast** was padding around out there and was coming back to get me. I just wanted to run! The feeling was overwhelming. I wanted to get away from that place as fast as I could! I stood up, and then the strangest thing happened: I started talking to myself out loud. **"Wayne," I said to myself, "If you run, you're gonna trip and fall and hit your head and be the next victim."** For some reason it calmed me down. I took a breath. "Get the water," the voice said. I got both water bottles. "Get the lights." I got both flashlights, but I was so rattled I couldn't make them work.

I started walking in the dark, only a few stars to light my path. I thought I knew the way out, but after a while the trail started getting steeper and steeper, and pretty soon I was down-climbing a vertical face. Again, the voice spoke to me. **"Wayne, you're gonna get to a place where you can't go down and you can't go up, and you're gonna fall to your death."** I climbed back out and went in a different direction. Pretty soon I rounded the shoulder of Hallett Peak, and there was Tyndal Glacier. Thank God! I knew exactly where I was. I sat down and drank some water and somehow got the flashlights working. After a while I started walking down Flat Top Mountain Trail, a three-hour trip, with both lights on, jabbering to myself out loud all the way. I finally got to the police station in Estes Park about two in the morning. "I want to report a man killed by lightning on Hallet Peak," I said to the officer on duty.

A half hour later a ranger arrived and took my statement. Next day they flew a helicopter up to Hallett Peak and brought Glenn down. Two days after that I met his family. They were very understanding and didn't hold me responsible, although I did.

So, what happened up there that caused me such fright? Years later I was talking with a paramedic, and he suggested that my fear that something was coming back to get me was because I was super-juiced up on adrenalin. My amygdala—that little fight-or-flight part of my brain—was working overtime and causing me to imagine things! I can't think of a better explanation.

BEN FRANKLIN AND LIGHTNING

Invention of the Lightning Rod

Folklore has it that Ben Franklin discovered electricity one stormy June day in Philadelphia in 1752 using a silk kite, some string and a key. Alas, that story isn't true. Someone had already done that. What he actually discovered was a way to demonstrate the connection between lightning and electricity. If lightning had actually hit his kite, he probably would have been electrocuted. Still his experiment was fruitful. It led to his **invention of the lightning rod** which undoubtedly saved many a building from lightning strike and destruction.[175]

Old Ben also invented a device called **lightning bells** which would jingle when lightning was in the air.[176]

WORLDWIDE INCIDENCE OF LIGHTNING

Lightning strikes the earth around 44 times a second with an average duration of 0.2 seconds.

Lightning occurs all around the world, but more in some places than other. Factors affecting the frequency and distribution of lightning include ground elevation, latitude, prevailing wind currents, relative humidity, and proximity to warm and cold bodies of water. About 70 percent of lightning occurs over land in the tropics. The small village of Kifua in the mountains of the eastern Democratic Republic of the Congo receives the most lightning strikes, about 410 per square mile per year.

Other lightning hotspots include **Lightning Alley in Central Florida.**[177] The 244 average lightning strikes per square mile per year in that region accounts for the large number of lightning-related deaths there each year - the most in the U.S. The number in Colorado, where I live, is only 34.4 strikes per square mile, but we have the second most deaths in the U.S., probably due to so many hikers and climbers in the mountains.[178]

Most lightning strike injuries in the United States occur **between May and September.** One-third are work-related, one-third occur during recreational or sports activities, and one-third from other situations, such as being struck while indoors or on the telephone.[179]

Lightning usually occurs during thunderstorms, but it can also arise during dust storms, forest fires, tornadoes, volcanic eruptions, and even in the cold of winter, when the lightning is known as **thundersnow.** The North and South Poles have few thunderstorms and therefore the least amount of lightning.[180]

TYPES OF LIGHTNING

Scientists classify lightning into three categories, cloud to cloud, intra-cloud and cloud to ground.[181] As mountaineers, we are concerned only with the last one, which can kill us.

HOW LIGHTNING WORKS

In a nutshell, lightning formation begins when the earth heats up and causes water to evaporate and rise. The rising vapor collides with other water and ice droplets which creates a positive electrical charge at the top of the cloud and a negative charge at the bottom. At the same time a positive charge is built up in the earth. When the buildup of charges is intense enough, the negative charge at the bottom of the cloud links up with the positive charge in the earth and lightning is created. The positive charge may extend upwards from any point on earth, including from human beings.

TECHNO-SPEAK: Lightning occurs instantaneously, in a fraction of a second, in a series of discrete steps some of which are well known to science, and some of which are still murky. The scientific word for the study of lightning is *fulminology*.[182]

EVAPORATION AND CONDENSATION

The first step in the creation of lightning is the **evaporation of water** from the earth. Evaporation occurs when a liquid absorbs heat and changes to a vapor. Once the vapor is formed, it begins to rise into the atmosphere. As the vapor rises, the temperature in the surrounding atmosphere gets lower. As a result, the vapor loses heat and eventually returns to a liquid state in the form of droplets. This is known as the *dew point*.[183] The transformation of vapor into water droplets is called **condensation.** If the atmosphere is cold enough, the droplets freeze into tiny crystals of ice. The droplets and the crystals then either fall to earth as what we see as rain, snow or sleet. They may also stay in the cloud or rise higher with updrafts of heated air.

FORMATION OF CLOUDS

As the sun heats the air near the ground, water vapor begins to rise into the atmosphere. Eventually these millions of water droplets and ice crystals aggregate into visible formations called **cumulus clouds**. These clouds continue to grow into the familiar towering shape. In the final stage of storm development, the top becomes anvil-shaped.[184] If you see these, be wary of lightning!

ELECTRICAL CHARGE FORMATION IN THE CLOUDS

The rising moisture droplets **collide with other droplets or with ice or sleet**—called *graupel*—already falling to the earth or located in the lower portion of the cloud, and an electron is knocked off. The newly knocked-off electrons accumulate in the lower portion of the cloud, giving it a **negative charge**. The rising moisture droplets which have just lost an electron carry a **positive charge** to the top of the cloud. Thus, there is **an electrical charge separation** in the cloud, negative on top, and positive on the bottom. When there is a charge separation, it is referred to as an *electric field*.

Also, a small positive charge develops in the lower part of the cloud which is important in determining which way the lightning flows, earth to cloud, or cloud to earth.

ELECTRICAL CHARGE FORMATION ON THE EARTH

As this process continues, the electric field becomes more and more intense. At some point, the **electrons on the surface of the earth beneath the cloud are repelled** and pushed into the earth by the strong negative charge in the lower portion of the cloud. As a result, the earth's surface below the cloud acquires a strong positive charge. The result is a negative charge in the bottom of the cloud, and a positive charge in the earth's surface below it, and the stage is set for a **lightning strike!**

INSULATING BARRIER

But the air between the negative charge in the bottom of the cloud and the positive charge on the surface of the earth acts as an **insulating barrier.** Lightning can occur only when **a conductive pathway** is found through the air. The electrical field creates this by causing pathways of air to 'break down' which allows electrical current to flow through the air from the negative cloud to the positive earth more easily. The broken-down air in the pathway is said to be **ionized** and is referred to as **plasma.** The plasma in effect creates a path that short-circuits the electric field. When the path is complete, lightning can occur.

STEP LEADERS

As the air continues breaking down, paths of plasma extending downward toward the earth are instantaneously created. The electrons in the air can move much more freely along these plasma paths, and thus **electrical current is able to flow** through the barrier of

Cloud-to-Cloud Lightning

insulating air. These plasma paths are called **step leaders**. The step leaders may expand and grow multiple branches and they may bounce around rather than going down in a straight line as they seek the path of least resistance though the air. This gives lightning its jagged appearance. Amazingly enough, the **step leaders are visible** with high-speed cameras as faintly purplish lines.

POSITIVE STREAMERS

At the same time objects on the earth begin responding to the strong electric field by putting out **positive streamers** toward the clouds above. These are also purplish in color and can be seen by high-speed cameras. Anything on the earth has the potential to send out a positive streamer, including human beings and animals. Once a step leader and a positive streamer meet, the **conducting pathway**, that is, the ionized air or plasma, is complete, and electrical current flows between the earth and the cloud as the charge separation is neutralized, and lightning appears.

RETURN STROKES

Every cloud-to-ground lighting flash is made up of one or more step leaders and one or more **return strokes**. The step leader is the initial step in the lightning flash and sets up the plasma channel which will conduct the electrical charge. Once a charged step leader connects with the ground, the return stroke occurs. It is simply the rapid discharge of electricity that has accumulated on the step leader. We see this discharge as a **flash of lightning.**[185]

SECONDARY STRIKES

Some lightning strikes appear to flicker or be stronger than other strikes. This is caused by the energy contained in the other **branch step leaders** to be diverted to the main step leader connecting to the positive streamer from the earth and results in the more lightning. This may cause multiple strikes in close succession. These are referred to as **secondary strikes.** If these secondary strikes are very close together—within milliseconds of each other—they give the lightning the appearance of a single strike; otherwise they cause the lightning to flicker.

LIGHTNING THAT JUMPS AROUND

A lightning strike doesn't stay in the place where it hits. It jumps around to nearby objects, including human beings, which provide a better path to ground, or discharge. **Thus "ground lightning"** is generated which can spread out from the point of impact or which can "splash" off other objects, like rocky overhangs, or even horses and hit individuals in its path.

Tree Split by Lightning

This huge surge of current is responsible for more injuries and deaths than the strike itself. This is why your group should spread out if overtaken by a storm and not get under a tree.

Lying flat increases your chances of being killed or injured by a ground strike as the lightning goes in one end of your body and exits the other end.[186]

CHARACTERISTICS OF LIGHTNING

THE HEAT OF LIGHTNING

Air is not a good conductor of electricity. It puts up a lot of resistance, and in doing so heats up, just like that red filament on your floor heater. The resistance is so high, in fact, that the air is heated to **50,000 degrees** Fahrenheit—five times the heat on the surface of the sun. When something that hot hits a tree, it makes the sap boil and vaporize, causing it to explode—a good reason not to get under a tree in an electrical storm.[187]

The average lightning strike contains **20,000 amps.** An arc welder uses 250-400 amps to weld steel.[188]

When lightning hits sandy soil, it can form a *fulgurite* (from the Latin word, *fulgur,* meaning light-ning.) The lightning actually melts the soil into var-

Fulgurite

ious shapes.[189] Fulgurites were featured in the 2002 movie, *Sweet Home Alabama* in which the hero, Jake, plants metal stakes in the sand during storms to attract lightning and create artistic fulgurites for his art studio. [190]

Although a lightning strike may contain from 100 million to 200 billion volts, its duration may be as short as 1/100th or 1/1,000th of a second. This extremely **short duration of exposure** explains why lightning strikes sometimes produce external burn injuries but minimal internal injuries.

THE COLOR OF LIGHTNING

Since our atmosphere is made up of nitrogen and oxygen, the lightning appears with a **brilliant blue-white color** the same way light appears in a fluorescent light tube. The color of the glow depends on the type of gas. If our atmosphere were made up of neon instead of nitrogen and oxygen, lightning would be white with orange edges.[191]

THE SPEED OF LIGHTNING

Lightning travels at **90,000 miles per second** (one hundred million feet per second). The **average thickness** of a bolt of lightning is 1-2 inches.

Lightning is usually found in towering, **cumulonimbus clouds**.[192]

BALL LIGHTNING

Ball lightning has been around for centuries. It is usually observed during thunderstorms— and sometimes before or after—as a floating sphere which varies from the size of a pea to several meters in diameter. It varies in color from blue to orange to yellow. Some observers have reported a hissing sound and an acrid odor. **Scientists do not agree** on what causes ball lightning or even that it is lightning.[193]

ST. ELMO'S FIRE

St. Elmo's Fire—also called a *corona* charge—is named after the patron saint of sailors. It is sometimes confused with ball lightning. It is a bright blue or violet glow and can appear like fire in some circumstances. It is most often seen on tall, sharply pointed structures such as masts, spires, and chimneys, and on aircraft wings or nose cones, but it can also appear on leaves and grass, and even at the tips of cattle horns. Often accompanying the glow is a distinct hissing or buzzing sound. It is seen during thunderstorms, when high voltage differentials are present between clouds and the ground.[194] Realistic depictions of St. Elmo's fire appeared in the 1956 movie, *Moby Dick,* with Gregory Peck as Captain Ahab.

THE SMELL OF LIGHTNING

That "clean" smell in the air after a thunderstorm is **ozone**—scientifically known as *trioxygen*—since it is composed of three oxygen atoms. Ozone has a strong smell that is often described as similar to that of chlorine.

Ozone is dangerous and in high concentrations and can destroy cells in your lungs. That's why you will occasionally hear an ozone alert announced over your radio, and individuals with compromised lung function are advised to stay inside.[195]

CLEAR SKY LIGHTNING

Clear sky lightning is lightning that occurs when there are no clouds visible. In the mountains a thunderstorm can be hidden and not visible in an adjacent valley.

The same is true in open areas such as large lakes or open plains where the storm is on or near the horizon. There may be some distant activity which results in a local strike. These are often referred to as **a bolt from the blue.**[196]

THUNDER

Thunder is created when lightning passes through the air. The lightning discharge heats the air rapidly and causes it to expand and then contract quickly. This rapid expansion and contraction create the sound wave we hear as **thunder.**

Since light travels faster than sound, you will see the lightning flash much sooner than you hear the related thunder. You can figure out how far away the lightning is by counting the seconds between the lightning flash and the sound of the thunder. The sound travels about a mile in five seconds, so counting" "one-one-thousand, two-one-thousand," and so on, you can determine approximately how far away the storm is.[197]

Be careful. It can be difficult to relate a particular thunderclap to a particular lightning flash. If you get it wrong, the storm could be closer than you estimate.

You can hear thunder for up to ten miles away, or less if conditions are windy, or a storm is raging.[198]

When you listen to thunder, you'll first hear the thunder created by that portion of the lightning's path that is nearest you. Then you'll hear the sound from the lightning's path that are farther away. Since the sound waves start from multiple points all along the length of the lightning's path, the origin of the sound of the thunder will be at varying distances and can generate a rolling or rumbling effect.[199]

Thunder is not harmless. If you are close enough to the lightning strike, you can feel the shock wave. As it passes, it shakes the surroundings and can injure you.

Since lightning can strike **ten miles** from a thunderstorm, if you hear thunder, you are probably within striking distance of the storm.[200]

LIGHTNING CREATED BY VOLCANOES

Volcanaoes can create lightning in much the same way clouds do. The **tiny particles** that make up a volcanic plume are tightly packed together. When they are ejected from the volcano, they rub against each other just like the water droplets and ice crystals in a cloud and become electricaly charged. As the charged particles ascend, the positive ones become separated from the negative ones. When the charge separation becomes great enough, lightning results.[201]

Walking across a rug in your socks has the same ffect. It creates static electricity which is discharged when you touch a door knob.

LIGHTNING STRIKING IN THE SAME PLACE TWICE

Contrary to urban myth, lightning often strikes the same place repeatedly, especially if it is a tall, pointy, isolated object. The Empire state Building in New York City is hit an average of 23 times a year.[202] And a U.S. Park Service Ranger, Ray Sullivan, was struck by lightning seven times![203]

LODESTONES

The movement of the electrical charges in the lightning produces a magnetic field. If the lightning current path passes through rock, soil, or metal, it can become permanently magnetized. This effect is known as *lightning-induced remanent magnetism*. Lodestones are magnets found in nature which were caused by lightning.[204]

TARGETS OF LIGHTNING

A lightning bolt can strike anywhere, including on humans and animals. Whether an object is metal or not makes absoutely no difference on where lightning strikes. Mountains are made of stone but get struck by lightning all the time.[205] However, touching or being near metal objects such as fences, railings, bleachers, or vehicles is risky when thunderstorms are nearby. If lightning hits it, the metal can **conduct the electricity** a long distance and electrocute you.[206]

LIGHTNING AND WATER

Lightning Striking Water

Lightning can **strike water** as well as more solid objects. When it does, the water acts as a conductor and the lightning radiates out in all directions. Swimming in a mountain lake during a thunderstorm can be fatal if lightning hits one part of the lake and spreads to you. You would have the same issue on a beach since the lethal radius of lightening is 600 feet, according to the National Oceanographic and Atmospheric Administration. Leave the beach and take shelter if you hear thunder or see lightning. Leisure activities such as hiking and climbing in the mountains accounted for 61 percent percent of lightning deaths during the years 2006 through 2019. Of those **35 percent were water-related**: occurring while in a boat, swimming or on the beach.[207]

LIGHTNING AND AIRPLANES

Lightning can hit your plane as you are flying over the mountains. Most aircraft skins consist primarily of aluminum, which conducts electricity very well and assures that the lightning current will remain on the exterior of the aircraft. Some modern aircraft are made of advanced composite materials, which by themselves are significantly less conductive than aluminum. In this case, the composites contain an embedded layer of conductive fibers or screens designed to carry lightning current.[208]

The body of the airplane acts as a **Faraday cage**. A Faraday cage is an enclosure can block electromagnetic fields, including those generated by lightning. It is formed by a covering of conductive material, or by a mesh or screen of such materials.

Plane Struck by Lightning

Faraday cages are named after scientist Michael Faraday, who invented them in 1836. He observed that the excess charge on a body resided only on the body's exterior and was not conducted to anything enclosed within it. In the case of an airplane, the body absorbs the lightning strike, so it doesn't hit the passengers.[209]

FIVE WAYS LIGHTNING STRIKES PEOPLE[210]

DIRECT STRIKE

A person struck directly by lightning becomes a part of the pathway of the lightning to the earth. Part of the current moves over the surface of the skin—a *flashover*—and another portion of the current moves through the core of the body, usually through the cardiovascular system and the nerves.

Direct strikes are responsible for 3 to 5 percent of lightning deaths.[211]

GROUND LIGHTNING

When lightning strikes the earth or anything on it, it doesn't stop at the point of impact. Much of the energy travels outward from the point of the strike along the surface of the ground. Ground lightning causes about 50 percent of all lightning deaths and injuries and kills many farm animals.[212]

SIDE FLASH

A side flash—also called a side splash—happens when lightning strikes something near the victim and then jumps to the victim. This usually happens when a victim has taken shelter under a tree. Side flashes are responsible for 30-35 percent of lightning deaths.[213]

CONDUCTION

Contrary to popular belief as metal does not attract lightning, but it can conduct electricity, metal provides **a pathway on which the lightning can travel**. Whether inside or outside, if you are in contact with anything connected to metal wires, plumbing or metal surfaces that extend outside, you are at risk. This includes anything that plugs into an electrical outlet, water faucets, bathtubs, showers, corded phones and windows and doors. Conduction is responsible for 3-5 percent of deaths by lightning.[214]

Rock climbers and peak-baggers should be aware that a **wet rope** can be good conductor and should always stay away from fixed ropes in a storm and not be tied in to each other.[215]

STREAMERS

Streamers radiate upward from the ground as the downward-moving leader gets near to the earth. Typically, only one of the streamers will make contact with the leader as it approaches the ground and provide the path for the return stroke, which flashes brightly. Streamers are responsible for 10-15 percent of deaths from lightning.[216]

WARNINGS OF LIGHTNING "IN THE AIR"

*Hair Standing on End from
Lightning in the Air*

Having your hair stand on end may seem hilarious in the moment, but it is actually a warning that lightning is "'in the air." This is because the negative base of the lightning in the clouds repels electrons in your hair causing the ends, which have become positively charged, to become attracted to the negative charge in the clouds.[217] The same is true when your fishing gear hums or your jewelry buzzes. This is an indication of immediate and severe danger. It's time for everyone to spread out and head down the mountain without delay!

INCIDENCE OF LIGHTNING STRIKES ON HUMANS

In the United States between 1989 and 2018 an average of 43 persons per year were killed by lightning—about 10 percent of those hit. The other 90 percent did not all escape unharmed. Many were left with varying degrees of disability.

FACTORS CONTRIBUTING TO DEATH FROM LIGHTNING STRIKE

There are several factors which contribute to death by lightning strike.

LACK OF APPROPRIATE KNOWLEDGE

Some individuals don't know the weather patterns in the area. Others are unaware that hair standing up on your arm means "lightning is in the air." Still others think that getting under a tree, an overhang or an open shelter in a rainstorm is safe.

VULNERABILITY OF THE ACTIVITY

Some activities such as boating, sailing, or peak climbing are riskier than others because there is no shelter in the event of a lightning storm.

INAPPROPRIATENESS OF THE TIME

In some locations the weather is predictable. In Colorado there is usually a short afternoon rainstorm around five o'clock every day in the summer. Good practice says that peak-baggers should be on top and coming down by noon to avoid these squalls.

UNWILLINGNESS TO POSTPONE OR CANCEL ACTIVITIES

It is particularly hard to postpone or cancel events because of bad weather. This is especially true of planned events involving lots of people like weddings or ball games.

BEING UNAWARE OF APPROACHING STORMS

In some instances, it is difficult to know of on-coming storms because the surrounding mountains hide the clouds and the thunder. Also, background noise, such as rushing water, occasionally masks the arrival of the storms.

INABILITY AND UNWILLINGNESS TO GET TO A SAFE PLACE QUICKLY

Despite adequate warnings, some individuals refuse to seek safety even though there is obviously a severe storm is in the offing. Others wait too long and when they finally do decide to leave, it is too late.

WHAT IT FEELS LIKE TO BE STRUCK BY LIGHTNING

Gretel Ehrlich in her book, *A Match to the Heart*, describes what it feels like to be struck by lightning:

> I woke in a pool of blood, lying on my stomach some distance from where I should have been, flung at an odd angle to one side of the dirt path...my voice didn't work. The muscles in my throat were paralyzed and I couldn't swallow...I had trouble seeing, talking, breathing, and I couldn't move my legs or right arm. Nothing remained in my memory—no sounds, flashes, smells, no warnings of any kind...The pain in my chest intensified and every muscle in my body ached...It started to rain. Every time a drop hit my bare skin there was an **explosion of pain.** Blood crusted my left eye. I touched my good hand to my heart, which was beating wildly, erratically. [218]

As in all first aid protocols, your first and continuing concern should be for **scene safety.** If the storm is continuing to rage, it may not be safe for you to try to attend to the lightning victim. As we have seen, despite folklore to the contrary, lightning **can** strike twice in the same place.[219] Multiple videos on YouTube document lightning striking quickly and repeatedly, no doubt inducing a fear of lightning, or as it is scientifically known, *astrophobia*.

FIRST AID FOR LIGHTNING VICTIMS

SCENE SAFETY

First aid protocols for lightning injuries and casualties are well-studied in the field of medicine called *keraunomedicine*.

REVERSE TRIAGE

Do not be afraid to touch a person who has been hit by lightning. They do not retain an electrical charge.[220]

In the case of a **multiple casualty** lightning strike event, if a victim has a pulse or is breathing, there's a good chance that he will survive the strike injuries. Therefore the patients in respiratory and cardiac arrest should be treated first.[221] This is referred to as *reverse triage*.

CARDIOPULMONARY RESUSCITATION (CPR)

Cardiopulmonary arrest, although rare, is usually the cause of death from a lightning strike. The heart will often automatically start to beat again after it is stopped by a lightning strike, however the victim may still not be breathing. Although normally a victim who is not breathing is sufficient cause to start CPR, it is important to take a minute to try to find a pulse. If one is found, only rescue breaths will be necessary, but you should assign someone to continue to monitor the victim's pulse to be sure it does not stop later.

The **survival rate** for lightning strike victims is about 10 percent.[222] Case studies show that survival rates for lightning strike victims may be higher than that for victims of heart disease or blunt force trauma. This is because the lightning strike victim may still have a healthy heart, whereas in other cases the underlying cause of the heart attack, such as a clot, is still present.[223]

CPR should be started as soon as you can safely enter the scene and **continued**

without interruption until the victim recovers from the shock of the lightning strike and heart beat and breathing begin again.[224] Since it may be some time before this happens or rescue arrives, you should ask passersby for help and begin to organize a long-term effort as soon as possible. This would preferably consist of multiple individuals on each side of the victim who will take turns doing chest compressions until tired, and one person at the victim's head administering a rescue breath every five seconds. The person providing rescue breaths should use a CPR mask, in one is available, unless it is definitely known that the victim is disease-free.

Once started, CPR should not be stopped until a members of the rescue team are kneeling beside the victim and are prepared to take over immediately with a bag-valve mask and chest compressions.

A *Sophie's Choice* situation arises when you are alone with **two or more victims** who have been struck by lightning, and more than one of them is not breathing. You may be able to resuscitate two victims at the same time by positioning one victim on each side of you and doing chest compressions simultaneously with one hand on each chest, and alternating rescue breaths, but this will be very difficult and require extraordinary stamina to continue for any length of time. Hopefully, someone would come by who could help. If there are more than two victims, you will have to choose, and don't beat yourself up afterwards for your decision, no matter what the outcome or criticism from others.

ENTRANCE AND EXIT WOUNDS

Once the victim's cardio-pulmonary function is determined or started again, you should perform a secondary, focused examination of his entire body. Entrance and exit wounds, if any, should be covered with a bandage in accordance with the usual first aid protocols. Be sure to look under clothing and shoes for injuries such as broken bones.

BURNS—OTHER SKIN EFFECTS

Lightning may cause **steam burns** when sweat or rainwater vaporizes and thermal burns from clothing set on fire or belt buckles or jewelry superheated from the lightning. These should be removed if it can be done so safely.

Lightning bolts have 30,000 or more volts, but it's not the voltage that is so important. It is how long the lightning stays on your skin. If your skin is dry, it will have more resistance, so it will take longer for the lightning to pass through you, and the burn will be more intense. But if your skin is wet, it makes a good conductor, and the lightning will pass more quickly.[225] Lightning conducted on the skin is referred to as a *flashover.*

Lighting also causes burns which leave a strange pattern of traces on the skin. These tree-like traces, which resemble **feathering or ferning**, are called *Lichtenberg figures.* They are formed when *capillaries* underneath the skin rupture from the lightning strike. They usually appear within hours of being struck by lightning, and they tend to disappear within a few days.[226]

Burns should be covered with a bandage, preferably sterile, to protect the wound from infection.

SECONDARY TRAUMA—FALLING OR GETTING FLUNG

The lightning strike can cause muscles to contract quickly and strongly, which may cause the victim to fall down or throw himself as much as several yards. Severe spinal injury may result, and spinal immobilization should be a regular part of patient management in lightning strikes.[227] Any trauma that are found should be bandaged and splinted as appropriate before transport.

SECONDARY TRAUMA—FLYING OBJECTS

The lightning strike can also cause debris to be blown away from the point of impact which can injure those nearby. These should be treated in accordance with appropriate protocols for lacerations, bruises, and broken bones.

TREATMENT FOR SHOCK

As in any trauma, the victim should be immediately treated for shock. Because of the likelihood of rain, it is particularly important to try to keep the victim dry and maintain her body temperature. This can be challenging, however covering her or shielding her from the weather can be accomplished with jackets, sleeping bags, tents, and so on. Also dealing with the underlying pathology, such as bandaging entrance and exit wounds, splinting fractures of extremities, and reassuring the victim once she regains consciousness are all part of the standard shock protocol.

OXYGEN

If available, oxygen should be administered to the strike victim through a nasal cannula at 3 liters per minute.

TRANSPORT

Victims should be transported to a hospital for further evaluation as soon as practicable.

SYSTEMIC INJURIES

Lightning can cause systemic injury to every part of the body and are far too numerous to mention here. These are for the most part not amenable to first aid at the site of the lightning strike. They must be triaged and treated at an advanced care facility like a hospital. But to give you a general idea of what can happen, I refer again to Gretel Ehrlich's *A Match to the Heart*, in which she describes how the electronic current from a lightning strike can impair almost every organ.

As millions of volts of electricity pass through the body, brain cells are burned, "insulted" or bruised, which can result in cerebral edema, hemorrhage, and epileptic seizures. Passing down through the body, electricity hits the soft tissue organs—heart, lungs, and kidneys—causing contusions, infarctions, coagulations, or cellular damage that can lead to death. Tympanic membranes in the ear sometimes burst from the explosion of thunder, and cataracts develop if the flash has been intensely bright. [228]

POST-ELECTROCUTION SYNDROME

Post-electrocution syndrome is "a group of cognitive and emotional pathologies resulting from a lightning strike." They include losses in, among other things, the ability to work, cognitive ability, depression, phobic withdrawal, loss of memory, initiative and concentration, loss of learning and loss development ability.[229]

LIGHTNING SAFETY

Now that we have a graphic idea of the damage lightning can cause to the human body, it's a good time to talk about how to avoid lightning.

PLAN AHEAD AND START EARLY

Check out the weather forecast for the area you are going to be in as well as surrounding areas, including for the next few days if you are going to be camping. Figure out how long it will take you to drive to the trailhead or bike path and give yourself 10 or 15 minutes when you get there to get **organized and equipped** to move out. Then add in the amount of time needed to arrive at your destination. Don't underestimate! Allow for the slowest member of the group, who should go first to keep the group from stretching out. Understand that for a really long day, you may be leaving in the early morning. Don't fight it! Sunrises are beautiful!

HAVE WEATHER AWARENESS

Keep an eye on the horizons—all horizons. In my state, Colorado, the weather usually comes from the northwest, but occasionally we get an upslope wind that comes from the southeast. As often as not these winds bring a deluge of rain and are very dangerous. If you have a weather app on your smart phone, consult it periodically. If you sense lightning danger, come down immediately. Things will **not** get better.

Again, if you notice your hair standing on end or hear your gear humming, there is lightning in the air, and you are in extreme danger. You should get down as quickly as possible—immediately!

START DOWN BY NOON

You should arrive at your destination and be coming down or returning by noon.

DON'T BE RELUCTANT TO TURN AROUND

If you see bad weather coming in, don't be afraid to turn around. The mountain will be there tomorrow. Bad weather includes a distant storm. Lightning can strike as much as ten miles from the storm site.[230]

SPREAD OUT

On the way down, if you are in or anticipating bad weather within 10 miles, spread out—way out! Put the fastest hikers first so you don't bunch up. Remember, ground lightning can travel as much as 100 feet and kill you.[231]

AVOID TALL OBJECTS

Avoid tall objects on the way down, like trees or rock formations. On treeless hillsides keep in mind that you will be the tallest object in the area. Avoid the top of the hill, if possible.

CAVES AS SHELTERS

Retreating into a cave is safe as long as you are not near the entrance where the lightning can jump from the top of the entrance to you and be conducted to the ground.

Also, don't stand in water or touch metallic handrails, or a wet rope, all of which can conduct the electrical charge from the lightning. And be sure to avoid touching the walls or ceiling of the cave if you are near the surface.[232]

SHELTER UNDER THE SHORTEST TREES

Trees can provide shelter from the storm, but not if they are the tallest in the area. Look for a group of shorter trees, but still spread out. And take note of any tree that may have previously been struck by lightning. It may be a **local hot spot** and in danger of another strike.[233]

AVOID OPEN SHELTERS

Most of us will head to the nearest man-made shelter in the event of a storm. But that could put us under the highest structure in the neighborhood and increase the likelihood of getting hit by lightning—like standing under a tree. In addition, don't stand under an open porch. The lightning can jump from the top of the porch to you and complete the lightning circuit.

SHELTER INSIDE A VEHICLE

If you are able to reach the trailhead, immediately **shelter in a car, truck, or bus** made of metal, provided it has a hard top. Stay inside and do not touch any of the metal parts of the vehicle during the storm or for 30 minutes after it appears to have passed.

A metal vehicle is essentially a Faraday cage and protects passengers from electric charges, such as lightning as long as the occupants are not in contact with electrical devices like the radio or the metal of the vehicle itself.[234] The rubber tires of a vehicle provide no protection.

SHELTER INSIDE A HOUSE

A safe place during a storm or when lightning could be present is inside a house or other building. You should not use telephones with cords. The lightning could hit the telephone line, travel down the cord and strike you. Cellphones and cordless telephones are okay.[235] Also **avoid plumbing**, including toilets. Don't take a bath, shower or even wash your hands during an electrical storm and don't stand by a window.[236]

IF THE STORM OVERTAKES YOU

If the storm overtakes you, get as low as possible—a ditch or defile would be best. Crouch, feet together. Lightning can go from one leg and to the other with serious consequences, so it is important that your feet are touching.[237]

Don't lie down! A nearby ground strike can run from one end of your body to the other to complete a circuit and kill you. If you are on a horse or bicycle, get off to reduce your height. Don't touch or be next to your bike while it is standing. The metal will not attract lightning, but it will provide an efficient conduit for the lightning from you to the ground.

LIGHTNING SUPPORT GROUPS

Lightning strike survivors often must deal for years and possibly a lifetime with the long-term results of their injuries. In these cases, it would be helpful to contact a support group such as Lightning Strike & Electric Shock Survivors International, Inc. It is a non-profit support group whose mission is "to provide a resource of continuous support and education in health and well-being for **survivors of a lightning strike and their families.**"[238]

— CHAPTER 4 —

AVALANCHE

On April 20, 2013, a group of experienced backcountry skiers and snowboarders assembled at Arapahoe Basin Ski Area in Colorado for a seminar on avalanche safety. Ironically, within hours five of them would be dead—killed by an avalanche! The sixth member of the party, almost completely buried, was rescued four hours later.[239]

The group had been thoroughly briefed by one of the victims, a certified avalanche safety instructor, about the dangerous conditions in the back country that day, particularly in the Sheep Creek Drainage where they were going. A series of storms had dumped several feet of new snow on a weak base layer deposited earlier in the season. They thoroughly discussed the avalanche warning published by the Colorado Avalanche Information Center that day and decided on what they thought was a less risky route. They were aware that only two days earlier a backcountry skier had been killed in an avalanche near Vail Pass further west. Only a few hundred yards from the parking lot, the group emerged from the trees into an open alpine area beneath a dangerous, north-facing slope. The six spread out, 50 feet apart, as they traversed below the slope and headed toward a small stand of trees. Three of the party had reached the trees when they suddenly heard a loud "wumph" —the sound of an avalanche breaking loose. The rest of the group ran for the small stand of trees, but the avalanche overtook them within seconds. It was 219 yards wide—more than two football fields—and 8 feet deep at the fracture line.[240] They didn't have a chance.

Five of the six were completely buried One was found 12 feet below the surface. The survivor was able to breathe but was literally frozen in place where he remained until rescuers arrived hours later. They found two of the victims buried next to him, although the survivor couldn't reach them. All the victims had activated their avalanche transponders, which helped rescuers find them, but too late to save all but one of them. Several group members were wearing Avalungs, breathing devices, but none were found in use. Also, two of the victims were wearing avalanche airbags, safety devices designed like water wings to help victims "float" on top of the onrushing avalanche.[241] Inexplicably, neither of them had exposed the ripcords that would have allowed them to trigger their airbags and possibly save their lives.[242]

THE FREQUENCY OF AVALANCHES

Avalanches are not rare. They occur thousands of times all around the globe and kill about 150 people a year. The large number of victims in the Sheep Creek Drainage disaster is by no means the biggest. The 1999 Galteur, Switzerland avalanche killed 31 people, all of whom thought they were safe in the so-called "green zone."[243] And just as tragic, 33 rescue workers were killed by a second wave of snow , known as a **hang avalanche**[244], in the mountains of eastern Turkey in February 2020.[245] The largest, however, was the Huascarian, Peru avalanche, which wiped out an entire village and killed an estimated 22,000 people.[246] An earthquake had caused a gigantic landslide, which in turn triggered the avalanche. Total dead in the disaster was estimated at upwards of 70,000.[247]

Avalanches were employed as a weapon in World War I when artillery shells were fired at snowpacks to trigger slab releases which swept away thousands of enemy soldiers.[248]

PARTS OF AN AVALANCHE

Avalanche Track

An avalanche has three main parts. The **starting zone** is where unstable snow can break loose from the surrounding and underlying snow and begin to slide. Starting zones are usually found on the upper part of slopes, but they can occur anywhere, even much lower down. Once in motion, the avalanche flows down an **avalanche track.**

Avalanche tracks which occur repeatedly over a given area are often visible where large swaths of trees are missing from a slope or where there are gullies forming **avalanche chutes** with little or no vegetation.

The **runout zone**, or **deposition zone** as it is sometimes called, is at the bottom of the avalanche track or avalanche chute where the snow and debris finally come to a stop and are deposited.

As the avalanche comes to a halt, it solidifies into **concrete-like snow,** making it difficult for victims and rescuers to dig out. The hardened snow in the Sheep Creek Drainage avalanche imprisoned the only survivor and prevented him from digging himself out even though he could move one arm. He lay, immobilized, for four hours until rescuers found him by following the signal from his transceiver.

CHARACTERISTICS OF AN AVALANCHE

In its simplest form, an avalanche is a mass of snow sliding or flowing down an incline when the weight of the snow, also known as "the load," exceeds the bond which holds it to the underlying layer. When that happens,

WUMPH!

A heavy slab has collapsed a weak, underlying layer, and down it comes, sometimes hard and fast, sometimes slow, and sometimes white and fluffy, but always potentially deadly.

Avalanches typically occur on slopes with an incline of between 30 degrees and 45 degrees—referred to as the *angle of repose*—although in various forms they can occur on slopes with a lesser incline. Steeper slopes tend to not hold the snow and therefore don't always form the snowpack which can result in an avalanche.[249] A 30-degree slope does not appear very steep, and this poses a hazard to unknowing skiers and hikers who do not realize the slope's potential for disaster. Wintertime and early spring are when most avalanches occur, but they have been recorded for every month of the year.[250]

Slab avalanches have been clocked at over 80 miles per hour,[251] so it's impossible to outrun one, even on a fast snowmobile. A small avalanche might be only a small shifting of loose snow called a **sluff,** whereas a large avalanche may carry 300,000 cubic yards of snow, or more—enough to fill 20 football fields ten feet deep.[252] Their power rivals that of a tsunami, and they can easily take out forests and buildings.[253]

DYNAMICS OF AN AVALANCHE

A snow-covered slope holds many secrets. To the typical back country traveler, it is a beautiful, pristine phenomenon of nature, but to the avalanche expert it has a larger, more complicated story to tell.

WEAK LAYERS

Avalanche slopes are in fact a combination of layers of snow, each layer deposited by a separate snowfall, and each layer having unique characteristics. Different storms create different types and amounts of snow and snow layers. Snow that has fallen onto an existing snowpack can quickly change into unique crystal types which are determined by changes in temperature and exposure to the sun. Even a deeply buried layer can continue to morph as changes in temperature seep slowly through the snowpack and heavier snow pushes down on lower layers. A weak layer is created when snow crystals are shaped in ways that prevent them from bonding tightly together.[254]

One of these weak layers, often found at the very bottom of the snowpack, is **depth hoar**. Contrary to popular understanding, as long as the ground has an insulating blanket of snow, it is almost always warm—near freezing—even with extremely cold air temperatures. When the temperature difference between the ground and the snowpack is substantial, the snow vaporizes upward, a process called *desublimation,* and refreezes, creating brittle, spiky, faceted snow, known as **depth hoar.** Depth hoar can support a lot of weight, but it is not strong enough to stop a heavy layer above from breaking loose and creating an avalanche.

You can tell if snow is depth hoar if you try to form a fistful of depth hoar grains into a snowball and the grains just fall out of your palm like sand. The snow crystals don't bond well enough to hold together.

Faceted hoar layers can also be found in the upper part of the snowpack where the snow has melted and refrozen. This so-called surface hoar might later become the weak layer on which other snow falls, and which ultimately fractures when the accumulated snow load becomes too great.

TECHNO-SPEAK: "When there is a big temperature gradient over a snowpack—warmer in some places and colder in others—water vapor moves from 'the relatively warm snow to the relatively cold snow and changes the recipient snow crystals, making them grow larger. They grow into faceted, square looking, crystals with poor bonds. Facets that develop near the ground are called **depth hoar.** Most avalanches occur when a stronger, denser layer called a slab forms on top of one of these weak, sugary layers."[255]

ICY OR CRUSTED LAYERS

An ice layer or crust may form when the surface has melted and refrozen which provides a smooth sliding service for snow which accumulates on top of the frozen layer later.

TYPES OF AVALANCHES

SLAB AVALANCHES

A slab avalanche looks like a cohesive block or slab of snow cut out from its surroundings by fractures, including a fracture at the top, or **crown fracture**; fractures on the side, or **flank fractures**; and a fracture at the bottom, also known as the **staunchwall**. Slabs can vary in thickness from a few centime-

Result of a Crown Fracture in a Slab Avalanche

ters to three meters or more.[256] Slab avalanches result when a cohesive snow layer on top of a weak layer of fractures and slides down the slope. The avalanche slab may give way because the weight of the snow load is too much for an underlying weak layer to support, or it may start because of a trigger [See **Avalanche Triggers** below].

Also, a **wind slab** can be formed by blown snow accumulating.[257] These are especially pernicious because they can accumulate a deep and heavy layer of snow.

Slab avalanches are extremely dangerous and kill the most people affected by avalanches each year.[258]

LOOSE SNOW AVALANCHES

Loose snow sliding down a mountainside is called **sluff**. Loose snow avalanches usually start from a point and spread out as they descend; because of this they are often called **point release avalanches.** Few people are killed by loose snow avalanches, and, unfortunately, the back country travelers tend to minimize their danger. In fact, houses have been completely destroyed by loose snow avalanches, and they can carry you over cliffs, into crevasses, or bury you in a **terrain trap** such as a gully or a tree well. Low danger does not mean there is zero danger!

POWDER AVLANCHES

A powder avalanche is made up of a powder cloud on top of a dense avalanche, such as a slab avalanche. The cloud is usually formed from fresh dry powder. It can move quickly, exceeding 190 miles per hour, and it can continue to flow long distances at the bottom of a slope and even uphill for short distances.[259]

WET AVALANCHES

Wet avalanches often occur when the weather warms up or when the sun or rain cause water to percolate through the snowpack and create weak layers of snow. A typical wet avalanche doesn't move very quickly, typically between ten and twenty miles per hour, because of the friction between the surface of the avalanche track and the water-saturated avalanche, but they are very heavy and can still be devastating.[260]

GLIDE AVALANCHES

A snowpack is said to glide when the entire snowpack slices down the slope. Much like a glacier, it moves because melt water lubricates the ground under it and allows the overlying snowpack to slip slowly down the slope. Usually, the glide moves too slowly to cause any damage, but on occasion it may release and become a catastrophic glide avalanche.

SLUSH AVALANCHES

Slush avalanches usually occur in the northern latitudes like the mountain ranges in Alaska. They are unusual because they occur on slopes as gentle as 5 to 25 degrees. When water saturates the snowpack, it loses its strength and cohesion and turns to slush. The resulting slush often runs long distances on very gentle terrain. Very few people are killed by slush avalanches.[261]

ROOF AVALANCHES

As unlikely as it may seem, people have actually been buried by a snow avalanche sliding off of a roof. Specific tools such as long-handled rakes have been designed and are available commercially to clear roofs with deep snow. Tapping on the ceiling under a steep snow-laden roof may also cause the snow to slide off. Be sure no one is in the impact zone when you attempt to clear the roof.

AVALANCHE TRIGGERS

In addition to failure of a weak layer, or the presence of an icy layer, avalanches may be started by a variety of triggers, both naturally occurring, and human caused.

ICEFALL TRIGGERS

Glaciers flowing over a cliff form what is known as an icefall. The falling chunks of ice can break away loose snow below or trigger slabs to form an avalanche. Icefall avalanches kill few people, mostly climbers who are in the wrong place at the wrong time. And that's exactly what happened in the well-known Khumbu Icefall at the bottom of the Khumbu Glacier on Mt. Everest. On April 14, 2014, an ice avalanche on the glacier was triggered by the fall of a giant serac, that is, an ice tower, which killed sixteen climbing Sherpas.[262]

EARTHQUAKE TRIGGERS

The 2014 ice avalanche on Mt. Everest is not the largest. The record was set by a devastating avalanche triggered by an earthquake on Mount Pumori in Nepal eight kilometers to the west of Everest; it measured 7.8 on the Richter scale. The avalanche wiped out the base camp, killing 22 people, and injuring many more. It left at least 61 climbers stranded on the mountain until they were rescued days layer by helicopter.[263]

CORNICE FALL TRIGGERS

Snow cornices are **formed by winds** blowing snow over the downwind side of a ridgeline. The cornice hangs out over the slope below. Eventually they break off when they become too heavy with snow or when a person or animal walks on them, trigger-

Cornices Waiting to Fall

ing an avalanche on the slope below. Cornices don't kill many people, mostly those venturing too close to the edge. It pays to be careful. Cornices have a tendency to break off further from the edge than you expect.

Cornices are occasionally used to advantage by climbers who intentionally trigger them to test the stability of the slope below or to intentionally create an avalanche to clear out an escape route off a ridge.[264] Be careful!

SNOW FALLING FROM TREES

Falling chunks of snow from trees are common natural avalanche triggers.[265]

WIND TRIGGERS

Sustained average winds have the potential to trigger soft slab avalanches. A sustained period of high wind and high precipitation occurring at the same time are predictive of a developing avalanche hazard.[266]

HIKER AND BACK COUNTRY SKIER TRIGGERS

Hikers and back country skiers are involved in many avalanches each year, most of which they survive. Those who are killed usually die in an avalanche that they or someone in their party triggered. The person triggering the avalanche does not need to be on the slope. He can trigger an avalanche from the bottom of the slope or even in the runout zone.

SNOWMOBILE TRIGGERS

Snowmobiling is great fun for more and more individuals and families every year. Cruising along a snowy trail on a sunny, blue-sky day can be intoxicating. The problem arises when snowmobilers venture off the trails onto snow-laden slopes where they die in avalanches triggered by themselves or someone in their group.

Any slope over 25 degrees can potentially slide, and the fastest snowmobile cannot outrun a slab avalanche. Avalanche conditions generally are found on slopes from 30 to 45 degrees. Unfortunately, these are exactly the slopes hard-core snow-mobilers love to ride, particularly those who are addicted to **high marking** or **high lining.** This refers to the practice of climbing steep slopes with a snowmobile to attain the highest position or get over the top. In their efforts they often trigger an avalanche. It is one of the **most dangerous things** you can do on a snowmobile and accounts for over 60 percent of avalanche deaths involving snowmobilers.[267]

NOISE TRIGGERS

Contrary to popular belief, noises such as yelling, yodeling, or the sound of a snowmobile will not trigger avalanches. Research has shown that only the loudest sonic booms under the most sensitive avalanche conditions might be able to trigger a slide.[268] Avalanches may also be triggered by landing helicopters,[269] although it is not clear whether this is from the sound of its engines or the downwash from its rotors.

AVALANCHE MITIGATION

Avalanche mitigation refers to man-made devices such as berms and barriers to protect fixed facilities like buildings and roadways, and devices installed to measure snowpack depth and composition and to report avalanche activity.

EXPLOSIVE DEVICE TRIGGERS

Avalanche mitigation includes firing mortars, light howitzers, and recoilless rifles into a snowpack near an expected fracture line to start an avalanche. Explosive packs and grenades have also been employed, but they are somewhat ineffective and dangerous to use since they have to be thrown onto the snowpack by hand. Where explosive devices, like howitzers, are repeatedly aimed at the same place on a slope, they are often permanently fixed in place. This allows them to be fired without aiming at night or during storms.[270]

GAZEX® TRIGGERS

Gazex® is an avalanche control system that uses specially constructed exploder devices built at areas of recurring avalanche activity to set off avalanches at controlled times. The exploders detonate a mixture of oxygen and propane from the buried tube structures. The force triggers the avalanche.[271]

AVALANCHE DAMS

To reduce the threat of avalanches **earthen and concrete "dams"** are often constructed across known and potential avalanche tracks. These are designed to absorb the avalanche flow or deflecting it away from protected areas.[272]

SNOW NETS

A **snow net** is a barrier using a wire net strung between metal poles that are anchored by strong wires. Snow nets are installed on steep slopes to keep avalanches from starting. During the winter, the net fills with snow as it accumulates on the slope rather than breaking loose and causing an avalanche.

STEEL FENCES

Steel fences are also employed. In Galteur, Austria, after the 1999 disaster, steel fences were constructed on all mountainsides above the village to break up hold back snow in areas where unstable snowpacks could form.[273]

REFORESTATION

Slab avalanches will not happen on slopes with enough dense tree cover—about 400 trees per acre on steep slopes and half that amount on gentler slopes.[274] Spruce and fir trees with branches frozen into the slab are a much more effective anchor than a tree with a few low branches such as an aspen or a lodge pole pine.[275]

Global warming has caused forests in many parts of the world to dry out at an alarming rate which in turn has led to an increase in wildfires which have destroyed extensive forests. Many of the burned forests provided protection from avalanches for mountain villages below. After the trees die, they no longer provide effective anchors for the snowpack. A study in Switzerland concluded that reforestation could mitigate avalanches if small clusters of trees were planted on known avalanche slopes.[276]

With this in mind, many avalanche experts advocate planting new trees rather than building expensive avalanche dams and snow fences.

SNOW SHEDS

Where known avalanche chutes are found, snow sheds are constructed to provide a pathway for the snow over roadways, railways and pipelines. Snow sheds have to be extremely robust structures to absorb the impact and weight of tons of snow from multiple avalanches whose snow may remain for most of the winter.[277]

A Snow Shed, or Avalanche Protection Zone Tunnel

RADAR DEVICES AND AUTOMATIC GATE- CLOSING DEVICES

Permanently installed radar devices are now used to detect when an avalanche has begun on some known avalanche paths. Within seconds the device triggers a stoplight and closes a gate on roads running across the avalanche path. The devices also enable avalanche control services to get an idea of the size of the avalanche as well as determining whether a controlled blast has been successful, thus reducing the risk of carrying out avalanche control work on the snow field itself.

Additionally, radar is also useful in monitoring areas to make sure no people are in areas where a controlled released avalanches is about to occur if visibility is poor.[278]

AVALANCHE SAFETY PROTOCOLS

PREPARING FOR BACK COUNTRY TRAVEL

Avalanche safety begins with an avalanche safety class long before you put your first foot on the trail. You can participate in most outdoor sports without the benefit of instruction, but back country winter travel is different. The objective danger is quantum leaps higher than running, for instance, or hiking in the wilderness. Back country travel is more like rock climbing or paragliding. You need to know how to do it right. A simple mistake can cost you your life.

Avalanche safety classes and refresher classes are everywhere, including face-to-face classes and on-line versions. They typically last a day and are generally quite affordable. But whatever the cost, it's worth it. You will be hearing about the reality of back country risks from people who have been there, some for many years, and some who have seen their friends eaten up by killer avalanches. Pay attention to what they say, and don't fight the course.

You also want to be sure the others in your back country party have taken a class, or at least a yearly refresher course recently and will adhere to the protocols and lessons taught there. You will have a good idea whether or not your usual snow-mates qualify, but what if someone new shows up? Do you have some standards in mind for allowing that person to join the group? It's best to check newcomers out before the day you meet on the mountain. This is important. The newcomer may be the only available rescuer to find you and dig you out of the snow at the bottom of an avalanche field.

CHOOSING A ROUTE

In choosing a route, you should ask yourself several questions: Do you have confidence in the abilities of all members of your party, and are you and everyone else sufficiently conditioned for the rigors of the route you have chosen *plus* a margin of error? Are you all well matched in terms of speed and stamina? Are you sufficiently experienced in the techniques necessary to take on the chosen route? Do all have the appropriate equipment and necessary route-finding skills to get in and out, particularly in a sudden, blinding snowstorm? And are you and members of the party well-matched in your tolerance for risk-taking?

Also, are you starting sufficiently early to **finish before dark,** allowing for a margin of error? Does everyone know that you are going to start on time even if means leaving a late-arriving person behind?

IDENTIFYING AVALANCHE CONDITIONS

North American Public Avalanche Danger Scale Avalanche danger is determined by the likelihood, size and distribution of avalanches.		
Danger Level		Travel Advice
5 Extreme	4 5	Avoid all avalanche terrain.
4 High	4 5	Very dangerous avalanche conditions. Travel in avalanche terrain not recommended.
3 Considerable	3	Dangerous avalanche conditions. Careful snowpack evaluation, cautious route-finding and conservative decision-making essential.
2 Moderate	2	Heightened avalanche conditions on specific terrain features. Evaluate snow and terrain carefully; identify features of concern.
1 Low	1	Generally safe avalanche conditions. Watch for unstable snow on isolated terrain features.
No Rating		Watch for signs of unstable snow such as recent avalanches, cracking in the snow, and audible collapsing. Avoid traveling on or under similar slopes.
Safe backcountry travel requires training and experience. You control your own risk by choosing where, when and how you travel.		

Also, before hitting the trail you will want to check out the **local weather report** and the avalanche report for the area you are going to be in. Knowing what the weather is going to be for the next couple of days is a good idea, just in case you get delayed and a snow bomb or other severe weather blows in. Just such an event happened in Colorado on March 13, 2019. A snow bomb hit and in less than 24 hours the temperature went from a sunny 80 degrees to a frigid 30 degrees accompanied by snow 54 inches deep in some places, with winds up to 80 miles per hour, and with severe drifting. This was not a good time to be in the back country.

If the weather is windy, **heavy snow loads** may be developing in spots which could trigger avalanches. And recent, heavy snowfall could also increase the snow load on slopes on your planned route. On the drive to the trailhead, take note of the weather. If it is warm enough to cause melting, the risk of avalanche is greater. Also is there evidence of **recent avalanches** along the road?

The morning of your outing you will *always* want to look at the **latest avalanche report**. Daily reports are provided throughout the snow season by various agencies. A list of local agencies is available from the National Avalanche Center at avalanche.org. The United States and Canada use the North American Public Avalanche Danger Scale to rate the avalanche danger.

Again, keep in mind that avalanche warnings from these agencies are based on generalized information from wide areas using data which may be hours old. You always need to assess the hazard based on what you see on the ground. If local conditions are better, no harm no foul, just carry on, but if they are worse, adapt accordingly.

The North American Avalanche Danger Scale is your starting point each day, but *you* must make the final decision.

SAFETY PROCEDURES WHILE EN ROUTE

Take note while on route whether everyone is following established safety protocols and whether they have their transceivers and other gear activated. Maintain **global awareness**. Do you see the results of fresh avalanches or snow loading from recent snowfall or the wind?

If your skis are **sending out cracks** as you move along, the snowpack is showing a readiness to fracture and cause a slab avalanche. The sound of wumphs or sharp bangs means slabs are breaking up.

CROSSING A POTENTIAL AVLANCHE SLOPE

Avoid crossing slopes greater than 25 degrees. The foot of such slopes is just as dangerous. When possible, you should even skirt the run-out zone at the bottom for total safety, particularly when weather conditions and other indicators point to a high avalanche danger. Be wary of **terrain traps**, cliffs you could be swept over, or gullies you could be swept into.

On any slope, avoid skiing or hiking above each other. You might trigger an avalanche that could engulf your buddy.

If you can't avoid crossing an avalanche slope or below an avalanche slope, do so **one at a time**! Don't think that an interval, even a large interval, between individuals, will protect you if an avalanche starts racing down. **You will not have enough time to make it to safety**!

The National Avalanche Center offers a short, introductory video on avalanche danger on its website. Go to the Education page of the site and select Tutorial.

AVALANCHE SAFETY EQUIPMENT

In addition to appropriate foul weather clothing and the usual back country ten essentials, *all* members of your group should have appropriate safety gear. Keep in mind that not all avalanche safety gear is intuitive to use. Every member of the group should already have practiced with each item. When minutes count and stress levels are high, you do not want to be wasting time trying to figure out how to use your rescue gear.

AVALANCHE TRANSCEIVERS

Avalanche transceivers are worn close to the body within easy reach. They are designed to continuously emit a radio signal that can be picked up by the other transceivers in the area. Other members of your party with transceivers can switch them to "search" mode to **locate your signal** even when you are buried.

All transceivers today operate on the same international standard of 457 kHz, so getting the same brand and/or model as others in your group isn't required.

AVALANCHE PROBES

An avalanche probe is the essence of efficiency. It is simply a lightweight aluminum pole which can be broken down into several sections for ease of carrying, just like a tent pole. It is used to probe for buried avalanche victims either by itself or during a more focused search with an avalanche transceiver. They are light weight and strong enough to poke through hardened snow.

SHOVEL

This simple, ancient tool is crucial to a successful excavation of someone buried in an avalanche. Typically, lightweight and made of aluminum with detachable or telescoping handles for easy packing, they are indispensable, especially when ski poles or hands alone are ineffective to **move frozen snow rapidly** from around the victim. You should carry a shovel designed specifically for avalanche rescue or else risk having one too big or too small for efficient use.

AVALANCHE BREATHING SYSTEMS

This is a **breathing apparatus** that allows an avalanche victim to pull oxygen from the surrounding snowpack and continue to breathe much longer than he could without it. And it helps prevent an ice mask from quickly forming around the victim's face when he attempts to breathe under the snow.[279] One option is putting the mouthpiece in place before starting down or across dangerous-looking slopes.

AVALANCHE AIR BAGS

An avalanche airbag is a device similar to an inflatable Mae West life jacket which is designed to help victims keep themselves afloat near the surface of the slide. An airbag pack contains CO_2 or compressed-air cartridges which, when manually activated, inflate a large airbag or two attached to the pack. The airbag is deployed when the user pulls on the manual ripcord.

The airbag acts like water wings to help you rise to the top of the avalanche.

Airbags may be shaped like an upside-down "U" to help protect your head and neck.

Deployed Avalanche Airbag
(photo courtesy of Mammut)

Others take the form of a large pillow from the top of the bag. Dual airbags pop out on the sides of the pack.[280] Airbags start at about $500 USD, but what is your life worth?

SLOPE METER

This small device, also called an *inclinometer* or *tilt meter,* is used to determine the **angle of a slope** for avalanche probability. Determining whether a slope is within the 25-to-45-degree danger zone can be crucial to your safety. They will run from $150 to $200, but you can use them for a lifetime. Maybe your regular group can buy one together.

RESCUE KNIFE

A rescue knife is strapped to your chest and used to cut your way out if you get buried in an avalanche. If should be readily accessible—not carried in your pack—so you can reach it even if you are mostly frozen in place.

Frequent practice with all of these items, especially the avalanche transceiver, is critical to using them effectively in an emergency situation when minutes count.

SURVIVING AN AVALANCHE

IF YOU ARE CAUGHT IN AN AVALANCHE

Immediately pull the ripcord on your airbag, and make sure the mouthpiece to your breathing device is securely in your mouth. Attempt to "**swim**" on the top of the snow with your feet downstream, so if you run into a rock or tree, your legs will absorb the shock. If you get buried, try to protect your head and neck and make an air pocket around your face with your jacket. Roll into a ball to minimize the trauma to your extremities. If you can, thrust a ski pole toward the surface which might be visible to rescuers. When the snow stops moving, try to carve your way to the surface with your rescue knife.

IF SOMEONE ELSE IS CAUGHT IN AN AVALANCHE

If someone else is caught in the avalanche, **follow him with your thumb** at arms' length, and if he goes under the snow, continue following the snow down the slope with your thumb until the avalanche stops. The buried person will be somewhere in the vicinity of the area covered by your thumb. Then line your thumb up with some terrain feature on the other side of the avalanche. **Do not take your thumb off the targeted spot**! Tell the others you have a fix on the buried person and ask someone to make sure more snow is not coming down. If all is clear, start walking directly toward the terrain feature, following your thumb, until you get to the place where your thumb stopped moving. Next take a 360 degree look around for evidence of the buried person. If you don't see him, but find items of his clothing or equipment, scan the avalanche field on a line directly upstream and downstream from that point in the avalanche field. If you still don't see him, start the probing procedure you learned in avalanche class.

Do not run for help. The buried person has no more than 15 minutes to live under the snow, and you would not be able to rally a rescue party that quickly.

CAUSES OF DEATH FROM AN AVALANCHE

Death from an avalanche can come in four possible ways:

- Trauma

Being ground up in thousands of tons of rapidly churning snow and ice can cause multiple **blunt force and compression trauma**, especially broken bones in your extremities and concussion if a helmet was ripped off.

- Suffocation

If you haven't been killed by the trauma of the avalanche, within minutes of being buried an **ice mask** will form around your face from your breath, and you will soon suffocate on your own carbon monoxide.

- Hypothermia

On a bright, sunny day, you might have pulled your jacket off, and even gotten down to a single shirt when the avalanche hits you. Even if you are fully clothed, over a period of time, being buried in solid snow will drop your temperature to the point where **hypothermia sets in**. [See Chapter 5].

- Shock

The trauma from the avalanche and the cold on your body can cause **shock** which by itself can bring on death.

FIRST AID FOR AN AVALANCHE VICTIM

Whatever part of the victim's body you discover first, you want to work toward clearing his head so you can start rescue breaths. This may mean removing snow and ice to the point where you can get down next to the victim. Consider carrying a small

CPR mask to avoid the risk of catching something from the victim. They are available in all sizes for less than five dollars, including one you can hang on your keychain.

Continue to deliver a rescue breath every five seconds whiles others in your group dig the rest of the victim out. As soon as you have him positioned on his back, have the others see if they can **find a pulse**, either by palpating the radial artery in this wrist or the carotid artery in his neck. There is typically enough oxygen left in a person's system to keep his heart going for 8 – 12 minutes even if he isn't breathing, so he may still have a heartbeat if you started rescue breaths soon enough.

If the victim is not breathing on his own, and you cannot find a pulse, you need to have someone **start chest compressions** while you continue with rescue breaths every five seconds. If you or the others are injured to the point where chest compressions can't be administered using the hands, an alternative is to use your knee or even your leg with the ball of your foot over the victim's heart. This is an unconventional technique, and you won't find it in any first aid books, but the alternative is to let the victim die in front of you.

After about two minutes of chest compressions and rescue breaths, stop the compressions, but not the rescue breaths, and try to find a pulse. If you do find a pulse, stop chest compressions. You may have to continue rescue breaths if the victim does not spontaneously start breathing. Continue **to monitor the victim's pulse** every two minutes and start doing chest compressions again if you can't find one.

While you are doing CPR, others can attempt to **warm the victim** by placing clothing under and around him. In this regard, carrying several large chemical body warmers is advised. Two of these should be placed next to the victim's skin, as close to his heart as possible. Also place one on each side of his neck against his carotid arteries and jugular veins. This will assure that warmed blood circulates to wherever the autonomic nervous system thinks it should go.

Once the victim is stabilized, you may want to have someone lie down on each side of the victim - under a jacket or **reflective blanket** if available to transmit their body heat to him in an effort to forestall hypothermia and shock.

If the victim starts breathing on his own, you need to turn your attention to secondary trauma, such as broken arms and legs. The extent of your efforts depends to some degree on how extensive your first aid kit is. At the very least you should always carry **trauma shears.** These are very sharp scissors which can be used to cut away material to visualize a wound, and also to cut strips off the bottom of someone's shirt to use for bandages or materials for applying splints. A makeshift splint can be made from a twig or a section of the victim's probe. Remember: **Splint it where it lies**! Do not try to put the broken extremity back in its normal position.

If the victim regains consciousness, begin immediately to reassure him that rescue is on the way and that everything is going to be okay. Your demeanor and what you say to the victim is more important than you realize in forestalling shock. Avoid the frowns and high-pitched, anxious-sounding voice. Don't discuss the negative aspects of his condition within his hearing. Stay with the victim and try to keep him talking as a way of monitoring his condition. Ask him if he is cold. Ask him if he would rather lie down or sit up. If the latter, someone can sit behind him to provide a back rest.

Victims in emergencies sometimes are very comedic. This is their way of coping. Play along with them. And don't underestimate the healing power of the human touch. Touching the victim's shoulder, or just holding his hand has **tremendous therapeutic power**.

Once the victim is stabilized, and you know what you are dealing with you can send for rescue. Send at least two people, never one alone, particularly if conditions have turned nasty. Be sure they have enough gear for their safety, including a map and lights.

HUMAN FACTORS CONTRIBUTING TO AVALANCHE ACCIDENTS

Despite numerous avalanche awareness programs, improved safety gear and more thorough reporting of hazardous avalanche conditions over recent years, avalanche fatalities and injuries have not decreased. As a result, some researchers are looking to the **behavioral science** to understand the continuing death toll. Different attitudes among groups and individual personality types account provide some explanation for the varying incidence of avalanche accidents. For example, a study revealed that in 2008 a third of back country travelers in Utah were women, they accounted for only 3.3 percent of fatal accidents[281]

One can think of many attitudinal reasons for the continued history of fatalities and injuries. For example:

- Not consulting the local avalanche danger agency
- Ignoring the recommendations of the local avalanche danger agency
- Ignoring signs of avalanche danger in the immediate vicinity
- Not crossing on or under a dangerous slope one at a time
- Believing that previous incident-free trips to and through a particular area mean an avalanche will not occur there now
- Not carrying rescue equipment
- Not being practiced in using your rescue equipment
- Not activating your rescue equipment ahead of time
- Undertaking routes beyond the ability of all group members
- Relying on strength in numbers
- Succumbing to peer pressure
- Wanting to project a macho image
- Showing off
- Taking shortcuts through unknown territory
- Camping under a dangerous snowfield
- High-lining or high-marking
- Building a snow cave in a dangerous snowfield

It is sometimes difficult even for strong, self-actualized individuals to call out these attitudes with potentially fatal consequences. Planning ahead and knowing the people you go out with will eliminate many of the problems. But when the chips are down and you aren't sure whether to speak up or not, think about the experience of the five unfortunate victims who died on Loveland Pass.

— CHAPTER 5 —

HYPOTHERMIA

In the winter of 1847, a group of settlers found themselves stuck, starving, and freezing, in the Sierra Nevada Mountains on their way to a new life in California. They would later become infamously known as the Donner Pass Party for the area where many of them died. Recent snowstorms and huge drifts of snow had isolated the group in the pass with almost no food and no feed for their livestock.

A few brave individuals tried to continue the journey and contact people over the mountains who could send back a rescue party. They didn't get far when they were forced to stop. They constructed a make-shift tent of blankets to protect themselves from the elements, but for Patrick Dolan it wasn't enough. On the first night without a fire, muttering to himself, he tore off some of his clothes and ran out of the make-shift tent into the frozen night. A few hours later, after he stumbled back; the others pulled him back into the tent, babbling incoherently and nearly naked. He died later that night, a victim of severe hypothermia.[282]

DEFINITION OF HYPOTHERMIA

Hypothermia is generally defined as a **body core temperature below 95 degrees Fahrenheit** in humans. Most mountaineers have experienced mild versions of hypothermia, or at least flirted with it, without a problem, but it can also be deadly. It causes around 1,500 deaths a year in the United States, many of those in the mountains, the rest mostly on city streets.[283] Given that the norm for body temperature is 98.6 degrees F, most people are surprised at how little it takes to slip into this unhappy state which begins at 95 degrees F.

The term hypothermia began to be used therapeutically by the medical profession in the 1930s. As a result, the medical profession started referring to the non-therapeutic version we get in the mountains as *accidental hypothermia*. In this chapter though, we will continue to refer to it simply as hypothermia.

INCIDENCE OF HYPOTHERMIA

Although generally associated with cold weather, hypothermia can occur on a summer day if you are wet and subject to a breeze.[284] The effect is the same, to strip your body of essential warmth. I experienced this phenomenon one June day on Mount Evans, outside of Denver where I live. I had biked to the top—14,265 feet (4,349 meters)—just in time to see the last tourist heading down. I was alone. It was late in the afternoon, and the sun was setting over the adjacent mountains. The temperature almost immediately dropped into the mid-forties.

I was instantly cold. My short-sleeved shirt was soaked with sweat, and the thin shell I brought with me didn't provide much warmth as I started coasting back toward the gate and my car, 14 miles away. The wind immediately stripped away whatever peripheral heat I had left. "Painful'" is not too strong a word to describe the feeling, but there was no alternative. Either I puckered up and continued on, or I walked down, which would have taken me several hours. The choice was clear, but the effect of the wind—I was going 15 - 20 miles per hour—was excruciating.

After a while I came to a little rise in the road, and I started pedaling to keep up my momentum. And then... it felt like something was closing in around me, starting at the sides of my chest and moving around to the front. It wasn't painful, but it wasn't normal either. I thought I was having one of those painless heart attacks! I stopped pedaling and the strange sensation also stopped. I continued down, and then it happened again.

Fortunately, just about then a man in a truck pulled around the bend. I waved at him, but I was so stiff I lost my balance and fell off my bike. He helped me up and said those magic words, "Would you like a ride down?" The answer was all too obvious. He loaded my bike into the back of his truck and helped me in the front. Then he drove us down to the parking lot where he fixed me the best cup of hot chocolate I ever had!

So, what happened up there? I finally figured out that I was at least mildly hypothermic, and when I started pedaling my autonomous nervous system began diverting the cold blood in my extremities into my body core.[285] What would have happened if I had continued to pedal? I don't want to think about it.

THE HISTORY OF HYPOTHERMIA

Hypothermia has been known as a cause of death for many millennia, although it wasn't always called by that name. Herodotus mentioned the cold in his *History* in 492 BC. Hannibal was said to have lost 20,000 men to the weather when he and his elephants crossed the Alps in 218 BCE. And of the 400,000 soldiers Napoleon took to the Battle of Borodino in 1812, only 10,000 returned. Many were killed in battle, but even more succumbed to hypothermia on the trek home in the middle of winter, exhausted and underfed.[286] In more modern memory, hypothermia killed thousands of soldiers at Stalingrad in World War II, both on the German side and on the Russian side.[287] [288]

DIAGNOSIS OF HYPOTHERMIA

Hypothermia is typically diagnosed in the field by either the temperature of the affected individual or his symptoms. Body core temperature is the most accurate method, but rectal or esophageal thermometers for this purpose are typically not available to rescue crews, so oral, infrared or ear thermometers are used, although these are not as accurate.

Definitive diagnosis of hypothermia was limited until the mercury thermometer was invented by Daniel Fahrenheit in 1714. But it was a foot long and required twenty minutes to take a temperature. Finally, in 1866, a small thermometer was invented that required only five minutes to use. But an accurate determination **of core temperature** today requires a special low temperature thermometer. Most clinical thermometers do not measure accurately below 93.9 degrees F.[289]

Hypothermia may start with a mild loss of body heat and progress gradually through stages to a life-threatening level. Often people aren't aware that they need help, much less medical attention.[290] These stages are typically described as follows:

- **Normal Temperature** – 95 to 98.6 degrees Fahrenheit

The human body is a wonderfully complex and adaptable organism. Yet we are *homeotherms*—animals with a **steady core temperature**—and our ability to exist is limited to a surprisingly narrow range of temperature, that is, just a few degrees above or below 98.6 degrees F. Below this level, things begin to get uncomfortable, and we risk gradual death from hypothermia. [291]

TECHNO-SPEAK: We can thank our *hypothalamus* for orchestrating the system that controls our body temperature—the thermoregulatory system—and thus our core temperature, from moment to moment. Shivering is our body's first response to the cold. That causes our normal *basal metabolic rate* to increase by two to five times in an effort to **generate more heat**. The hypothalamus also strives for **heat conservation** by *peripheral vasoconstriction* or shrinking the size of our veins and arteries—to reduce heat conduction to the skin. The hypothalamus also initiates non-shivering *thermogenesis* (heat generation) by calling for higher levels of the hormone *thyroxine*, a product of the thyroid gland and also acts to increase the metabolic rate. It triggers the release of adrenaline as well, also known as epinephrine; it is the hormone produced by the adrenal glands that acts to increase blood flow to the muscles, the heartbeat and output of the heart and the blood sugar level.[292] But once the hypothalamus's capacity to keep our core temperature warm enough is overwhelmed, hypothermia begins to creep in.

- **Cold stressed** – 95 to 98.6 degrees Fahrenheit.

The individual is functioning normally, although some shivering may occur, and is able to care for herself. This is not a hypothermic condition.

- **Mild Hypothermia** – 90 to 95 F degrees Fahrenheit

At this temperature shivering increases and turns into what could better be termed a very unpleasant, even painful, shuddering. At the same time *tachycardia* (fast heart rate), and *tachypnea* (fast respiration) appear. Systemic indicators of mild hypothermia are high blood pressure and *vasoconstriction* (contraction of blood vessels) and low blood sugar.[293] Both of these are chronic conditions for some people, so ask the affected person if she suffers from Raynaud's disease or *hypoglycemia*.

At this stage, the person may also experience *cold diuresis*, which is the medical term for increased production of urine. It leads to an intense **need to urinate** and follows from vasoconstriction. When the body senses the cold, it starts to constrict the flow of blood to the skin to keep the warmth around internal organs. As a result, blood pressure increases because there is now the same amount of blood being pumped through a smaller amount of space in your veins and arteries. In response to the increase in blood pressure, the kidneys begin to filter out excess fluid in your blood to reduce the blood's volume and lower the blood pressure. The bladder fills, and the need to urinate arises.[294]

- **Moderate Hypothermia** – 85 to 90 degrees Fahrenheit

As hypothermia progresses, symptoms include noticeable mental status changes, such as confusion, slurred speech, and loss of fine motor skills.[295] You feel a tremendous urge to go to sleep which brings on the risk of freezing to death if you are outside.[296] Sleeping in a warm environment indoors is therapeutic and not harmful to a hypothermic victim, and should not be discouraged once you get all the information from him that you need.[297]

- **Severe Hypothermia** – less than 85 degrees Fahrenheit[298]

Death is likely.

- **Profound Hypothermia** – Some experts regard a core temperature of less than 75 degrees as profound hypothermia.[299]

As your body's temperature decreases, more physiological systems begin to falter. Heart rate, respiratory rate and blood pressure all decease dramatically. You will ultimately lapse into a coma and die of heart failure.[300]

PARADOXICAL UNDRESSING

As a person gets deeper and deeper into hypothermia, a strange phenomenon occurs: the sensation of being on fire. The desire to undress is overwhelming.

Around 85 degrees F., people who are freezing to death become disoriented and confused and often begin to take off their clothes. This is known as *paradoxical undressing.*[301]

One explanation for this bizarre reaction is that the **hypothalamus is so cold** that it is malfunctioning and sending the wrong signals to the peripheral vascular system, causing it to dilate and fill with warm blood. Another explanation is that the **muscles contracting the peripheral blood vessels** have become exhausted and relax, leading to a sudden surge of warm blood to the extremities, causing the person to feel overheated.[302]

Search and rescue teams report finding a trail of clothes leading to the hypothermic victim. As the victim froze, he took off his clothes and kept walking.[303]

TERMINAL BURROWING

Another strange result which often accompanies hypothermia is *terminal burrowing, also known as* the *hide-and-die syndrome.* In the final stages of hypothermia, the victim will try to shelter in small, enclosed spaces, such as underneath beds or behind furniture. Researchers suggest this is an autonomous process of the brain stem which produces a **primitive and burrowing-like behavior** of protection, like that seen in hibernating animals.[304] This is similar to some warm-blooded animals who will dig or burrow into a small, enclosed den to spend the winter. The tight quarters surrounding their bodies help to minimize heat loss.

FACTORS LEADING TO HYPOTHERMIA

Although cold is the main cause of hypothermia, other considerations may play a role:

- Wind chill

With enough wind the warm insulating layer of air that usually is in direct contact with the skin is carried away, leading to **wind chill.** The amount of heat blown away from the body is directly proportional to speed of the wind.[305]

- Altitude

If you hike, bike, ski or climb at a high elevation, there is less oxygen available to you, a condition known as *hypobaric hypoxia.* As a result, you will be able to **metabolize less oxygen** and therefore produce less heat, thus increasing the likelihood of hypothermia.[306]

- Exhaustion

Once you get tired and start to slow or stop exercising altogether, your rate of heat production falls dramatically, thus increasing the risk of hypothermia.[307]

Intense exercise can lead to what is known in the medical field as *thermoregulatory exhaustion* and to the rest of us as *hikers' hypothermia.* This is a syndrome involving extreme **prior physical exercise in a cold environment,** which leads to physical exhaustion.[308] This results in an impairment of vasoconstrictor responses to the cold, and shivering, the body's main responses to cold. [309]

- Insufficient fitness

Fitness may be important when individuals with a lower fitness level try to keep up with other group members who are more fit. Since most mountain activities are pursued in groups, the less fit are more likely to become fatigued and stop generating heat compared with their fitter companions.[310]

- Overheating

Paradoxically, overheating (*hyper*thermia) may ultimately lead to *hypo*thermia. This happens when the individual fails to keep a *thermal balance* between the heat generated by exercise and the venting off of excess heat by opening his jacket or shedding layers of clothing. As continued exercise generates more body heat, his insulated clothing traps the heating and inhibits the evaporation of sweat. As a result, clothing near the skin becomes saturated. When the individual stops moving, sweating may cease, but the wet clothing chills the person and adds to his heat loss.[311]

- Glycogen depletion, or hypoglycemia

Body temperature can drop after only a few hours as a result of exhaustion and glycogen depletion.[312] Glycogen can be maintained or restored by eating foods with a high carbohydrate content while in the mountains.

- Age – older individuals

Older people are more at risk for hypothermia because of their body's decreased ability to adjust to the cold. **Prescriptions** for pre-existing medical conditions and some **over-the-counter medications** can also increase their risk of hypothermia.[313]

- Age – children and infants

Infants and young children may not be able to communicate with adults about the cold, or they ignore it because they are having too much fun. Moreover, younger children may not know enough to dress properly in cold weather or to get out of the cold when they should.

Also, infants and children have a **greater ratio of body surface** to body mass, and therefore lose more heat.[314]

- Alcohol

In the past alcohol was thought to be helpful to hypothermia victims because it caused them to feel warm. What is actually happening is the alcohol causes **peripheral vasodilation,** which allows increased blood flow to the skin where it makes the individual feel warmer, but at the same time allows increased heat loss—right at a time when conserving heat is paramount.[315]

- Dehydration

Cold-induced diuresis, urination, vomiting, diarrhea, sweating and even the water vapor exhaled in our breath may lead to dehydration. The body needs **water to maintain normal functions**, but we tend not to drink as much in cold weather as in hot weather.[316]

- Head injury

Head trauma may cause interference with the body's ability to respond to the cold by limiting shivering or by allowing vasodilation and the escape of heat from the skin. If a person's level of consciousness seems more impaired than it should be with hypothermia, suspect a head injury; another possible cause is substance **overdose.**[317]

- Drugs

Opioids and some other drugs, including legitimate, prescription drugs, can interfere with the thermoregulatory response of the body to cold.[318]

- Body fat

Thin people lose heat more rapidly. Research has shown that higher body fat percentages provide higher tissue insulation during cold exposure.[319] All those pepperoni pizzas may save your life someday.

- Pre-existing medical conditions

Certain pre-existing medical conditions, such as diabetes, Parkinson's disease, and hypothyroidism, can affect the body's ability to regulate its temperature.

METHODS OF LOSING HEAT

Body temperature reflects the balance between heat production and heat loss. Heat is generated by cellular metabolism and lost by radiation from the skin and in water vapor from lungs during breathing.[320]

- Evaporation

Each breath we take **exhales moisture** in the form of warm water vapor. This is especially true in the mountains where the air is often dry. Carrying lots of water and drinking before you feel thirsty will help keep you hydrated.

- Radiation

Every inch of your skin radiates heat. Typically, we are mostly covered with clothing which inhibits heat loss from the skin. Many believe that one's head loses inordinate amounts of heat. In fact, your head represents only about 10 percent of your body surface, and it loses no more heat than other uncovered parts of the body.[321] This myth can be traced back to an experiment by the US Army in the 1950s in which volunteers were dressed in Arctic survival suits—except for their heads—and exposed to wintry conditions. Because it was the only part of their bodies left uncovered, the experimenters concluded that "most of their heat was lost through their heads." [322] Technically correct? Yes. Good science? Not!

• Conduction

Heat loss by conduction can be severe. Sitting on a metal ski lift chair or lying in the snow can take a heavy toll of heat. Being submerged in water or having saturated clothing is particularly good at conveying heat.

• Convection

Heat can easily be carried off by even a small breeze. Wind chill increases with wind velocity and can be just as harmful as an actual drop in temperature.[323]

HUNTER'S RESPONSE

A strange phenomenon called *hunter's response* may occur in individuals who frequently work in the cold, such as Norwegian fishermen or Inuit hunters. In freezing temperatures the surface capillaries on their freezing hands would periodically open to allow **warm blood** to flow into them.[324] Once the hands were warm again, *vasoconstriction* would occur, and the blood flow would shut down. The process would then repeat itself again and again.[325]

THE RELATIONSHIP BETWEEN FROSTBITE AND HYPOTHERMIA

As stated above, **peripheral vasoconstriction** which diverts blood to the core is one of the major ways the thalamus directs the body to fight hypothermia. However, without warm blood flowing to the extremities, their temperature is going to fall, giving rise to an increased potential for frostbite. [326]

On the other hand, evidence of frostbite, such as loss of feeling in the fingers, toes, cheeks, nose, or ears can be a warning of the onset of hypothermia.

INITIAL TREATMENT OF HYPOTHERMIA

The initial goal of rescuers in the field is to **keep the victim from getting any colder or wetter**. If possible, immediately get him under a makeshift shelter, even if it is just a blanket or ground cloth, to protect him from the elements. Until proven otherwise, assume that the victim is not able to generate heat and needs external warming to maintain his body temperature. Hopefully you will

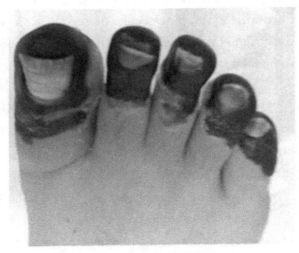

Severely Frostbitten Toes

have brought along several large **chemical body warmers**—the kind with sticky backs to hold them in place. Put two of these on the center-left of his chest, against his skin, to warm his heart and blood. His autonomous nervous system will direct the warmed blood to the places in the body where it's most needed: the heart, the lungs, and the brain. Also place one on either side of his neck to warm the blood passing through the carotid arteries and the jugular veins to and from the brain. These are large vessels which lie close to the surface and carry a lot of blood. Cover these with a scarf. Other warmers can go in his groin and armpits.

At the same time try to **wring out his wet upper body clothing**, if you can do this quickly without chilling him further. If you have found items of clothing which he has discarded along the trail—from *paradoxical undressing*—help him put these back on, together with any additional clothing you may have brought with you.

If you have **warm liquids** in vacuum insulated containers, have the victim begin sipping these to start the warming process from the inside and to restore body fluids lost through diuresis.

Next, put the victim in a 55-gallon plastic bag—the kind you find on construction sites. These are extremely helpful in protecting him from the elements and **preserving any residual body heat** while waiting for rescue to arrive. I always carry three of these on hikes, one to act as a bivvy sack for the victim, a second one, filled with leaves, pine needles or grass to act as a mattress and to insulate him from the ground or the snow, and a third one also filled with leaves, pine needles or grass to be used as a blanket for the victim.[327]

Keep the victim awake, if possible, until he is in a warm environment.

If the victim is unconscious, **assess him for breathing and pulse**. The American Heart Association recommends palpating for pulses for at least 30 to 45 seconds before initiating CPR to be sure there is no heartbeat.[328] In hypothermia cases the heart rate slows down tremendously and if you listen for only ten seconds, you might miss a heartbeat or two and start CPR on a slowly beating heart.

The victim should be moved to a warm place as soon as possible. It is best to extract the victim from the hypothermic environment in a horizontal position if you have the resources to do so. Even low intensity use of peripheral muscles, as in walking for example, should be avoided to minimize the risk of **core temperature afterdrop**. [329]

CORE TEMPERATURE AFTERDROP

Core temperature afterdrop refers to the continued cooling of a patient's core temperature during the initial stages of rewarming. The afterdrop is caused by the **return of cold blood from the extremities to the core due to peripheral vasodilation**. In other words, external warming of the victim or exercise causes his peripheral veins and arteries to dilate or open up, which allows the cold blood to flow inward to the victim's core, thus causing a further decrease of deep body temperature.[330] In addition, the opening of constricted peripheral vessels all at once as a result of rewarming can cause a sudden drop in blood pressure which may lead to *rewarming shock*.[331] Core temperature afterdrop is not observed in all hypothermic patients. It is more common in those who were rapidly rewarmed.

TECHNO-SPEAK: Severe hypothermia and inappropriate rewarming can have a negative impact on the autonomic nervous system by **causing impaired sympathetic cardiovascular control** after rewarming. This is a dysfunction that can cause rewarming shock.[332]

In severe cases core temperature afterdrop can lead to **post-rescue collapse**. In 1980, sixteen shipwrecked Danish fishermen were rescued after an hour and a half in the frigid North Sea. After being brought aboard the rescue ship, they walked to the hatch leading to a warm cabin below—and each one dropped dead![333]

Once the individual is rescued from the hypothermic environment, rewarming should be started as soon as possible. Rewarming techniques are divided into **passive external rewarming, active external rewarming**, and **active internal rewarming.**

PASSIVE EXTERNAL REWARMING

Once you get the victim into a warm, dry place such as a cabin or ambulance, you need to determine whether he is amenable to **passive rewarming**, that is, rewarming himself by generating his own heat. For this to happen, the victim must be able to shiver and to metabolize carbohydrates to create heat.[334] Would-be rescuers all too often will bundle up a severely hypothermic victim or cover him with blankets. This only insulates the victim from ambient heat.

Rewarming hypothermia victims is a slow process! Do not hurry. The goal is to restore the victim's body temperature and normalize all bodily functions without triggering **core temperature afterdrop.** It could take hours.

ACTIVE EXTERNAL REWARMING

If the victim is not able to generate enough heat to recover on her own, **active rewarming techniques** should be started:

- **Note that in all cases the victim's trunk should be rewarmed first, then the extremities** to avoid core temperature afterdrop.
- Remove wet clothing.
- Place the victim in front of a moderate heat source, such as a fireplace, or in the front seat of a vehicle with the heater on.
- Give the victim warm liquids, but not caffeinated coffee which causes heat loss.
- Place hot water bottles on the victim's chest, over her heart, and against the sides of her neck, being careful not to burn her with overheated water. The victim may have decreased feeling on her skin and not be able to tell you how hot the hot water battle is.

- Place a heating pad on the victim's chest.
- Exchange body heat with the victim in a "**hypothermic burrito**" by having the victim lie on a blanket or sleeping bag with a rescuer on each side of her, and then rolling them up in the blanket to create the appearance of a burrito. It helps to have the minimum amount of clothing on all three individuals to facilitate transfer of body heat. Expect to remain together for at least two to three hours, although other rescuers can be substituted from time to time.
- Give the victim carbohydrates to restore blood sugar which is necessary to support shivering and body metabolism.
- Continue to monitor the victim.
- Treat for shock.
  - Put the victim in a position of comfort.
  - Treat the underlying pathology—the hypothermia, and any trauma.
  - **Reassure the victim**. Talk to her and stay next to her; this also helps you monitor the victim. The importance of this can't be overemphasized as a way to combat potential shock.

ALLOWING THE VICTIM TO SLEEP

Many times, a hypothermia victim is overwhelmed by drowsiness and may want to fall asleep. If this happens while the person is still in a cold environment, she risks freezing to death.[335] In a warm environment, where the victim is being slowly re-warmed, there is no risk in allowing the victim to go to sleep, as long as you have gotten all the information from her that you need. To the contrary, sleep is therapeutic and can be helpful in the victim's recovery.

ACTIVE CORE REWARMING

In the old days, hypothermia was treated in the hospital in reverse order. The victim was doused first with snow, then ice water, cold water, and finally, warm water. The idea was valid—slowly rewarming—they just started in the wrong place. And it wasn't that long ago that they used to put a victim in a hot bath to recover. Not surprisingly, many had heart attacks and died as the cold peripheral blood migrated to the core and shocked the heart. Not a good outcome! Finally in the twentieth century more effective methods were adopted.

Active core rewarming refers to a **series of advanced techniques** administered in a medical facility such as injecting warmed intravenous fluids into the victim, rewarming the victim's blood, and irrigating the victim's body cavities, such as the abdominal cavity, with warmed fluids, among other procedures.[336]

Hospitals also employ all of the techniques in active external rewarming plus a device known as a *Bair Hugger* (invented by Dr. Bair) which looks much like an **air mattress hooked up to a hair dryer.** It is designed to pump warm air through tiny holes on the underside of the device which is then laid over the victim to slowly raise his core temperature.[337]

In all cases of hypothermia, extreme care should be taken **to move the victim as gently and as little as possible.** Jostling may increase risks of serious heart issues such as ventricular fibrillation and heart attack.

COLD SHOCK RESPONSE

Hypothermia sometimes accompanies another cold-related pathology called *cold shock response.* This usually happens when someone falls through the ice. The immediate shock of the cold water causes involuntary inhalation which, if underwater, can result in drowning, massive increase in blood pressure, and cardiac strain leading to cardiac arrest and panic. Within another 15 to 30 minutes *cold incapacitation* sets in and the individual loses use or control of limbs and hands for swimming or holding onto something, as the body protectively shuts down the peripheral muscles of the extremities to protect its core.[338]

I experienced **cold incapacitation** when I participated in the Cherry Creek Reservoir Triathlon south of Denver one hot summer day. I saw some people wearing wetsuit tops, but thought no more about it—until I hit the water. The shock of that cold water caused me to take a huge breath, and I started breathing on the very top of my lungs. I couldn't exhale all the way; I kept taking huge breaths even though I wasn't swimming very hard. I made it to the turn-around pylon when **my arms started getting heavy,** making it hard to keep swimming. I was last so there was no one else around except for a couple guys in a canoe who, fortunately, spotted me floundering around and somehow dragged me aboard. They took me ashore to the medical tent, covered me with a reflective blanket and gave me warm Gatorade. What would have happened if they weren't there? I don't want to think about it.

THE MAMMALIAN DIVING REFLEX

The *mammalian* diving reflex kicks in when you fall through the ice. As soon as the freezing water hits the *trigeminal nerve* of your face, your body begins to manage the lack of oxygen by selectively shutting down parts of the body not necessary for immediate survival. In effect you lapse into a **protective hypothermia** as soon as your core temperature falls below 95 degrees Fahrenheit. This phenomenon gives rise to the quaint old adage: "You're not dead until you are cold and dead."

From the rescuer's point of view this means that CPR must be started and continued until the victim is removed to a warm environment and recovers to a more or less normal body temperature—which may be several hours. In the meantime, you need to treat the victim with external passive rewarming measures. Also be sure to check for a pulse every few minutes which may re-emerge as the individual warms up.

TECHNO-SPEAK: Since the mammalian diving reflex shuts down aerobic metabolism in the body, and there is no blood flow, *lactic acid* builds up in the cells. If the body warms up too fast and a surge of lactic acid is suddenly released, it can acidify the blood to toxic levels. So, the challenge in the emergency room is to keep the blood flowing to move the lactic acid to the kidneys where it is expelled without letting it all rush to the body's core and to the heart. [339]

Stella Berntdsson at age 13 had the lowest known body temperature when she was pulled from under the ice in a lake near her home in Goteborg, Sweden. **She had no heartbeat**, but CPR was started in the helicopter on the way to the hospital. It wasn't until the next day that she started to show signs of life—a heartbeat. Twelve hours later she opened her eyes, and two weeks later spoke her first words. Today she is fully recovered.[340]

PREVENTION OF HYPOTHERMIA

Prevention of hypothermia is mostly a matter of common sense:

- Check out the weather.

Before going out, always **check out the weather** for the next two days, just in case you get stuck and have to spend the night. Remember that in the mountains the weather changes rapidly. In Colorado we have a saying, "If you don't like the weather, just wait ten minutes."

- Dress appropriately.

It's really fun to **hike up a Colorado 14-er**—a 14,000-foot mountain—in your shorts and tank top, but what are you going to do when it starts to rain? Or sleet? Or snow? All of which can happen in the mountains without much warning. And it will be cold anyhow when you reach the top and when you leave the trailhead early in the morning, so why not take some extra clothing? Dress in layers starting with a base layer that will wick the moisture away from your body. You want to be able to take off and put on clothing as needed to adjust to the ambient temperature, wind conditions, and your body heat. Also, be sure your cap or hat has a cord or chin strap to prevent it from blowing away in the wind.

- Carry appropriate equipment.

Even on a warm summer day the weather can turn ugly. Where I live, we usually get a summer rain squall late in the afternoon, so I always carry a plastic rain poncho. It is inexpensive and lightweight. I am also prepared, no matter what the weather, to spend a night if I go down. This means, I always carry a wool hat, balaclava, neck gaiter, extra shirt, jacket, gloves and three 55-gallon plastic bags, even on a warm summer day.

- Avoid excessive sweating.

On some days it seems like you are forever **taking off or putting on layers**, but it is worth the effort. If you don't and accumulate excess sweat, when you stop moving, it will continue to evaporate and can cool you to the point where you become hypothermic.

- Avoid getting wet.

Water carries off heat at least **30 times faster than air**.[341] Falling in a lake or stream and getting soaked can be life-threatening, especially if there is even a light breeze.

- Carry your cellphone and your satellite rescue device.

I used to hike with a person who thought carrying a cellphone "ruined the wilderness experience." Then he fell down and broke his ankle. It took several painful hours to hobble back to the trailhead instead of calling Search and Rescue and getting carried out. Meanwhile he got colder and colder. Luckily, his injury wasn't life-threatening, but what if your friend has a heart attack, and time is of the essence? Carry the phone.

- Avoid getting over-tired.

If you get over-tired, your body will not be able to generate sufficient heat from exertion or shivering later, when you need it to avoid hypothermia.

- Stay well-hydrated.

In the mountains, **the air is typically dry**, so we blow off moisture with every breath. Eventually we can become dehydrated which means lower blood volume and reduced ability to circulate warm blood throughout the body. Also, the typical hypothermia victim is at least mildly dehydrated from cold-induced diuresis.[342]

- Maintain blood glycogen.

Glycogen, or blood sugar, is the source of energy for our body. Unless replaced, it eventually diminishes to inadequate levels, leaving us unable to exert ourselves, or shiver to keep warm. **Consuming carbohydrates** on the trail is the best way to assure an adequate level of blood sugar. Carry a couple of candy bars for quick energy.

- Check each other out.

As previously noted, hypothermia is a stealthy killer. It creeps up on and us, and we are often unaware of what is happening until it is too late. To avoid this problem, **check each other out** from time to time, and don't ignore signs like slurred speech and diminished physical capability. Checking each other out means insisting at the trailhead that your companions wear the appropriate clothing and carry the appropriate gear too.

- Avoid alcohol.

See Factors Leading to Hypothermia above for a discussion of alcohol.

- Don't resist turning back.

The situation often presents itself that for one reason or another it is a good idea to turn back, short of your goal for the day. One of your group may be getting over-tired or hurt or showing signs of cold stress. In any of these events, do not be reluctant to turn back. The situation will probably not get better. You can usually come back on another day when it is safer to continue.

SHELTERS

Primitive Snow Shelter

Any shelter which protects you from the wind and snow and holds in some body heat is desirable. The Donner Pass Party used their blankets to put together a makeshift tent. Standard back country survival calls for construction of a snow cave. **Snow is a very good insulator** and will keep the temperature around freezing. Caution: Do not dig your snow cave at the foot of a slope that might avalanche. And if are able to build a fire in your enclosed space, be sure to put it out to avoid carbon monoxide poisoning while sleeping unless you have a chimney or stovepipe to vent the gases outside.[343]

LONG TERM EFFECTS OF HYPOTHERMIA

Severe hypothermia can result in organ damage and permanent medical issues, however, there's usually a good chance for complete recovery without long-term effects.[344]

PREGNANT WOMEN

There are only a few reported cases of pregnant women who were hypothermic in the mountains. In one case, not surprisingly, the heartbeat of the fetus of a hypothermic, pregnant woman was depressed until the mother was re-warmed.[345] Research has shown that being too cold for an extended period of time during pregnancy increases the risk of premature birth.[346]

ACCLIMATIZING

People who spend a great deal of time outdoors become **outdoor acclimatized.** These persons can withstand heat or cold extremes because their bodies have adjusted to the outdoor environment. Acclimatization usually occurs over a period of about two weeks in healthy, normal persons.[347]

FREEZING EXPERIMENTS BY THE NAZIS

The Nazis conducted freezing experiments at the Dachau concentration camp outside Munich in the early 1940s. The stated goal was to study hypothermia for the benefit of the armed services, but it's modern scholars think that these experiments were in reality brutal torture crimes conducted under the guise of medical science. There is still controversy whether data from the experiments has any validity and whether it is ethical for today's scientists to use data from torture crimes.[348]

PETS AND HYPOTHERMIA

Although bears and some other animals can survive extremely low temperatures for extended periods of time by replacing most of their internal water with *sugar trehalose* and inducing hypothermia, household pets, like dogs, cats and horses, cannot.[349]

A dog or cat might display symptoms such as tiredness, muscle stiffness, shivering, shallow breathing, and—if the hypothermia is severe—fixed, dilated pupils.[350] Also, if you see a dog sit down in the snow and start licking his feet, that is a sign that it is cold and hurting. Although water dogs like retrievers have specially-adapted coats which give them a high tolerance for cold, they can also become chilled, especially if they get wet and it is windy.

If all cases, if your pet seems more than mildly distressed, it should be immediately taken to a veterinarian.

Treatment of a pet with hypothermia is the same as treatment for a human, and as in the case of humans, be careful not to jostle it and possibly cause a heart attack.

Appendix A: Incident Report Form

Completed by _____ on _____.

Victim's name _____ Age____ Date _____

Time of incident _____AM/PM

Victim's address_____

Telephone_____

Mechanism of injury/Nature of illness _____

Time rescue started _____AM/PM

LEVEL OF CONSCIOUSNESS: A/O x ____ V P U

SAMPLE HISTORY

Signs and symptoms
Allergies
Medications
Past medical history
Last intake food/liquid
Events prior to incident

HANDS-ON PHYSICAL EXAM:

HEAD/NECK/SPINE:

Chest: Legs:

Abdomen: Arms:

Pelvis:

Time _____ AM/PM

Time _____ AM/PM

Time _____ AM/PM

VITAL SIGNS

Pulse rate   Pulse oximetry

Breath rate   Pupils

Skin   Temperature

Cap refill

CARE:

— ACKNOWLEDGEMENTS —

My deepest thanks to Jana Stephens and Natalie Bolton who offered many helpful comments on the content and presentation of this book.

My deepest thanks also to Maryann Karinch, without whose expert advice and endless patience this book would never have happened.

If you have any comments about what you read here, please send them to me at faroutfa@gmailcom. Also, I would enjoy reading about any experiences you may have had with the killers on the mountain.

— *Wayne Smart*

— AUTHOR BIO —

Wayne Smart is a licensed Emergency Medical Technician and an active hiker, climber, biker and skier. Based in Denver, Colorado, he has extensive experience in teaching wilderness and remote first aid across the state. Prior to becoming an EMT he practiced law for many years in Illinois and Colorado and taught at Front Range Community College in Fort Collins. In addition to teaching courses for his company, Far Out First Aid (FOFA), Wayne has an active mediation business helping individuals resolve divorce and workplace disputes. Since 1980, Wayne has made his home in Colorado, where he lives with his little dog, Buddy.

— PHOTO CREDITS —

— INDEX —

A

Acclimatization 29, 32, 38, 45, 112
  Acute mountain illness 42
Acetazolamide (Diamox) 38, 41, 43
Acute mountain illness 27, 28, 29, 119
  prevention 42
  treatment 38
Acute mountain sickness 28, 30, 33, 34, 35,
    38, 42, 44
Alcohol 19
  acute mountain sickness 31, 45
  hypothermia 100
Altitude-induced peripheral edema (AIPE)
    28, 37
Arizona coral snake 3
  avoiding 5
  fangs 3
  neurotoxic 3
  physical characteristics 3
Avalanche 71
  air bags 86
  dams 80
  depth hoar 75
  dynamics 74
  equipment, safety 82
  fences 80
  first aid 88
  frequency 72
  "human factors" contributing to 90
  mitigation 80
  parts of 73
  reports of 84
  snow nets 80
  snow sheds 81
  surviving an 87
  transceivers 85
  triggers 77, 77–80, 78–81, 79–82, 80–83
  types of 76

B

Blood
  effects of venom on 9
Brumation 4

C

Carbo-loading 43
Clear sky lightning 57
Cold shock response 107
CPR 16, 50, 64, 89, 104, 108

D

"Dead" snakes 14
Delayed symptoms 10
Depth hoar 75
Dexamethasone 42
Dogs and snakebite 24

E

Elderly and snakebites 13
Encounters with snakes 6
Envenomation 7, 9, 13, 15, 17, 20
  pathway in body 9
Evacuation 9, 13, 22, 23

F

Faraday cage 60, 69
Frostbite and hypothermia 102

G

Gamow bag 40
Gazex triggers 80
Ginko biloba 44
Groups, snakes in 6

H

Habitat 4
Hair standing on end 62, 68
Hibernation 4
High altitude cerebral edema (HACE) 35
High altitude flatus expulsion (HAFE) 38
High altitude pharyngitis/bronchitis (HAPE)
    37
High altitude pulmonary edema (HAPE) 36
High altitude retinal hemorrhage (HARH) 36
High altitude syncope 38

— ENDNOTES —

1   Steadman, C. (October 9, 2017). Hiker Dies After Snake Bites Him on Mt. Galbrait, *Golden Transcript*.

2   Western diamondback rattlesnake. (September 1, 2020). *Wikipedia*. Pg. 1.

3   Rattlesnake - Smell. (September 17, 2020). *Wikipedia*.

4   Urgent Care Evaluation for Snakebite Envenomation. (2018). *The Journal of Urgent Care Medicine*. Pg. 2

5   Crotalus viridis. (July 31, 2020). *Wikipedia*. Pg. 4.

6   Micruroides. (June 10, 2019). *Wikipedia*. Pg. 2.

7   Arizona coral snake (Micruroides euryanthus). *https://www.desertmuseum.org/books/nhsd_coral_snakephp*. Pgs. 1-2.

8   Coral Snake. (August 30, 2020). *Wikipedia*. Pg.

9   Coral Snakes: Color, Bites, Farts & Facts. *Live Science*. Pg. 2.

10   Micruroides. *Op Cit*. Pg. 2.

11   Arizona Coral Snake. (November 2, 2018). *Arizona Poison and Drug Information Center*. Pg. 1.

12   Lavonas et al. (2011). Uniform treatment algorithm for the management of crotaline snakebite in the United States: results of an evidence-informed workshop. *BioMedCentral Emergency Medicine 11:2*. Pg. 5.

13   Ibid. *Golden Transcript*.

14   Roberts, M. (May 18, 2018). Rattlesnake Season in Colorado. *Westward*, P. 3.

15   Micruroides. *Op Cit*. Pg. 2.

16   Rorabaugh, J. (2019). Soronan Coralsnake. *Tucson Herpetological Society*. P. 5.

17   Colorado Parks and Wildlife. *Rattlesnake Management – Stewardship Prescription*. Op cit. Pg. 8.

18   Merriam-Webster Dictionary. (2008). *Brumation*.

19   Phillips, C. et al. (2018). Snakebites and Climate Change in California, 1997-2017. *Clinical Toxicology*. P. 1.

20   Rorabaugh. *Op Cit*. Pg. 5.

21   Rattlesnake – Smell - Wik*ipedia. Op Cit*.

22   Steve Irwin. (July 16,2020*). Wikipedia*.

23   Colorado Parks and Wildlife. *Rattlesnake Management – Stewardship Prescription*. Op cit. Pg. 9. Https//www/extension.colostate.edu/topic-areas/natural-resources-coping-with-snakes-6-501/

24   Do Snakes Jump? (May 3, 2016). *Florida Wildlife Control*. http;//www:247wildlife.corn/snakejump.html.

25   Wildlife Removal USA.

26   Fry, O*p cit. Pg. 45, 77*+

27   Snakebite - Outmoded First Aid. (Edited July 30, 2020). *Wikipedia*,

28   Paniagua, D., Vergara, L.Boyer, L., and Alagon A., (January, 2017). Role of Lymphatic System on Snake Venom Absorption, Snake Venoms. *Springer Link*. Pg. 453.

29   (Roizes, L., and Weid, P., (December 15, 2014) Distinct roles of L-and T-type voltage-dependent Ca2+ channels in regulation of lymphatic vessel contractile activity. *Journal of Physiology*. Pg. 5409.

30   Helden, D.F., (December 15, 2014). The lymphagion: a not so 'primitive' heart. *The Journal of Physiology*, P. 5353.

31   Artzberger, S.M. (2014). Fundamentals of Hand Surgery – Overview of Lymphatic Anatomy Related to Edema Reduction. Pg 3.

32   Moore, Jr, J. and Bertram, C. (January 2015). Lymphatic System Flows, *Annual Rev. Fluid Mech*, 50:459-482, Pg. 465.

33   Howarth, D., Southee, A., and White, I. (November 30, 1994), Lymphatic flow rates and first-aid in simulated peripheral snake or spider envenomation. *The Medical Journal of Australia*. 16(11-12) 695-700, Pg. 695.

34   Fry. *Op Cit*. Pg. 49.

35   Lavonas *et al*. (February 3, 2011). Unified treatment algorithm for the management of crotaline snakebite in the United States. *BMC Emergency Medicine* 2011, 11:2, Pg. 8; www.biomedcentral.com/1471-227X/11/2.

36   Fry, B. Op cit. Pg. 33.

37   The third major type of venom, neurotoxic venom, is present in coral snakes which are not found in Colorado.

38   Boyd, J., (September 2007). Venomous Snakebite in Mountainous Terrain: Prevention and Management. *Journal of Wilderness and Environmental Medicine, Volume 18, Issue 3*. P. 193

39   Fry, B. *Op cit*. Pg. 48.

40   Cerato, M. and Andelt, W., Op cit. Pg. 6.

41   Andrew Vang, A. *Urgent Care Evaluation for Snakebite Envenomation*. The Journal of Urgent Care Medicine. https/www.jucm.com/urgent-care-evaluation-snakebite-envenomation, Pg. 3.

42   Mulder, E., Op cit. Pg. 5.

43   Lavonas, et al., *Ibid*. Pgs. 8-9.

44   Paniagua, D., Vergara, I., Boyer, L., Alagon, A., (January 2015). Role of Lymphatic System on Snake Venom Absorption. *Springer Science + Business Media*, Ch. 19, P. 454.

45   Wikipedia – Arizona Coral Snake. Pg. 3.

46   Cavazos, et al., (2012). Snake Bites in Pediatric Patients, a Current View S. Greene, *Hospita Universitario Facultiad de Medicina UANL, Mexico*. www.interchopen.com. Pg. 1.

47   Spyres, M.B. et al. (2018), Epidemiology and Clinical Outcomes of Snakebite in the Elderly, 56. *Clinical Toxicology*. P. 112.

48   Hayes, J. (February 6, 2018). How pregnancy can lead to death by snakebite. abc.net.au/news/2018-02-06/how-pregnancy-can-lead-to death-by-snakebite. P. 2.

49   Wikipedia. (October 30, 2019). *Aortal Compression Syndrome*. Snakebite during pregnancy: a literature review.

50   Langley, R.L. (March 21, 2010). Snakebite during pregnancy: a literature review. Wilderness Environmental Medicine. ncbi.nim.nih.gov/pubmed/20591355.

51   Roberts, M. Op cit. Pg. 6.

52   J. Boyd, J. Op cit. Pg. 6.

53   M. Cerato and W.F. Andelt, revised by M. Reynolds. (August 2014). Coping with Snakes, *Colorado State University Extension, Fact Sheet No. 6.501*. Pg. 1.

54   Cerato, M. and Andelt, W.F. Op cit. Pg.2

55   Suchard, J.R.,M.D. and LoVecchio, F., D.O. (January 17, 1999). Dead Snakes Can Be Lethal - Letter to the Editor. *New England Journal of Medicine*, Pp.340:1930.

56   Kilvert, N. (December 4, 2017). You've Just Been Bitten by a Snake. *ABC News – Science*. P.6.

57   Cerato, M. and Andelt, W.F. O*p cit*. Pg. 3.

58   Vang, A. *Ibid*. P 6.

59   Artaberger, S. (2014). *Fundamentals of Hand Surgery*. P.1.

60   Lavonas *et al*. Op cit., Pg. 5.

61   Campbell, B.T., Boneti, C. (July, 2008). Abstract - *Pediatric Snakebites: Lessons Learned form 114 Cases*, J. Pediatric Surgery, 43(7) Pp. 1338-1341.

62   Lavonas *et al*. Op cit. Pg. 5.

63   Andrew Vang, O*p cit*. Pg. 5.

64   Bryan Fry, *Op cit*. Pg. 76

65   Bryan Fry *Ibid*. Pg. 79

66   Bryan Fry, *Ibid*. Pg. 79

67   Bryan Fry, *Ibid*. Pg. 82

68   Bryan Fry, I*bid*. Pg. 47.

69   Warnell, D.A. Guidelines for the Management of Snakebites – 2nd Edition (2016). *World Health Organization – Regional Office for Southeast Asia.* Pg. 117.

70   Bryan Fry, *Op cit*. Pg.46.

71   Van Helden, D.F., J. Dosen, P.J., O'Leary, M.A., and Isbister, G.K., (2019). Two pathways for toxin entry consequent to injection of an Australian elapid snake venom, *Scientific Reports,* 2019:9:8595. Pg. 12.

72   Snake bite: coral snakes. (November 2006). National Institutes of Health. *https://pubmed. ncbi.nlm.nih.gov/17265902/*.

73   Bryan Fry, *Op cit*. Pg. 81

74   Mayo Clinic Staff. Snakebites: First Aid. mayoclinic.org/first-aid/first-aid-snake-bites/ basics/art-20056681. p. 2.

75   Suction for venomous snakebite: A study of "mock venom" extraction in a human model. (2004). *Annals of Emergency Medicine.* Vol. 43, Issue 2, Pgs., 181-186.

76   Fry. *Op cit*. Pg.78.

77   Michael B Alberts, M.B., Shalit, M., and LoGalbo, F. (February 2004). Suction for Venomous Snakebites. *Annals of Emergency Medicine,* Volume 43, Issue 2, Pgs. 181-186.

78   Fry, *Op cit*. Pg. 85.

79   Parker-Cote, J. Op cit. (April 29th, 2018). The Role of the Lymphatic System in System Toxicity of Snakebites, *Journal of Pharmacology and Clinical Toxicology.* Pg. 1.

80   Fry. Op cit. Pg.75.

81   Fry. Op cit. Pg. 79

82   *Ibid.* Pg. 81.

83   Warnell, *D.A. Op cit*. Pg. 63.

84   Fry. *Op cit*. Pg. 76.

85   Fry. *Op cit*. Pg. 55

86   Matt Schudell (June 18, 2011). Bill Haast Dies at 100, *The Washington Post*.

87   Snake Venom – Immunity – Among Other Animals. (August 3, 2020). *Wikipedia,* "Immunity"

88   Methow Valley Veterinary Hospital. (2020). methowvalleyvethospital.com/ rattlesnake-vaccine-faq

89   horseandman.com/handy-tips/what-happened-to-my-horses-face/06/22/2014.

90   Fry. I*bid*. Pg. 88.

91   Krakauer, J. (September 1966). Into Thin Air. *Outside Magazine.* Pg. 1.

92   Hackett, P.H., Shim, D.R. (October 18, 2019). Travelers' Health, Chapter 3, Environmental Hazards & Other Noninfectious Health Risks – High Altitude Travel & Altitude Illness. *Centers for Disease Control and Prevention*/ Pg. 3.

93   Altitude Illness. (2016-18). *Institute for Altitude Medicine at Telluride.* Pg. 1.

94   U.S. Army Medical Series. *Op Cit.* Pg. 43.

95   U.S. Army Medical Series. *Op Cit.* Pg. 1.

96   Ntlzar, N., Strohl, K., Faulhaber, M., Gatterer, H., Burtscher, M. (July 1, 2013). Hypoxia-Related Altitude Illnesses. *Journal of Travel Medicine,* Volume 20, Issue 4. Pg. 250.

97   Altitude Illness. *Institute for Altitude Medicine at Telluride. Op Cit*. Pg. 1.

98   Hackett, P., Shlim, D.R. (October 18, 2019). High Altitude Travel & Altitude Illness. Pg. 5.

99   Murdoch, D. (March 18, 2010). Altitude Sickness. *BMJ Clinical Evidence.* Pg. 1209.

100   Auerbach, P. (February 6, 2016). *Medicine for the Outdoors – 6th Edition.* Pg. 313.

101   Pulse Oximetry, *Johns Hopkins Medicine – Health Home Treatments – Tests and Therapies.* Pg. 2.

102   U.S. Army – Altitude Acclimatization and Illness Management. *Op Cit.* Pg. 28.

103   Mayoclinic.org/diseases-conditions/raynauds-disease/symptoms-causes/syc-20363571.

104   U.S. Army – Altitude Acclimatization and Illness Management. *Op Cit.* Pg. 1.

105   Roach, R.C., Hackett, P.H., Oetz, O., Bartsch, P., Luks, A.M., MacInnis, J.J., Baillie, J.K. (2018). The 2018 Lake Louise Acute Mountain Sickness Score, *High Altitude Medicine & Biology,* Vol. 19, Number 1. Pg. 5.

106   Altitude Illness. *Institute for Altitude Medicine at Telluride. Op Cit.* Pg. 1.

107   Auerbach, P.S., (February 6, 2015). *Medicine for the Outdoors - 6th Ed,* Pg. 307.

108   Pre-existing Medical Conditions at Altitude. (2016). *The Institute for Altitude Medicine.* Pg. 7.

109   Advice for Women Going to Altitude. *UIAA.* (September 5, 2018). *UIAA - International Climbing and Mountaineering Federation.* Pg. 2.

110   U.S. Army – Altitude Acclimatization and Illness Management. *Op Cit.* Pg. 56.

111   Wise, M. (2010). Travel Health Guide, *Firefly Books.* Pg. 73.

112   U.S. Army – Altitude Acclimatization and Illness Management. *Op Cit.,* Pg. 57.

113   Luks, A.M., Swenson, E.R., Baertsch, P., (2017). Acute High Altitude Sickness. *European Respiratory Review.* Pg. 3.

114   Altitude Illness. The Institute for Altitude Medicine. *Op Cit.* P. 3.

115   U.S. Army – Altitude Acclimatization and Illness Management. *Op Cit.* Pg. 57.

116   Hypoxia-Related Altitude Illnesses. *Op Cit.* Pg. 250.

117   Medicine for the Outdoors. *Op Cit.* Pg. 310.

118   Altitude Sickness. *The Institute for Altitude Medicine. Op cit.* Pg. 4.

119   Altitude Sickness. *The Institute for Altitude Medicine. Op cit.* Pg. 7.

120   U.S. Army – Altitude Acclimatization and Illness Management. *Op Cit.,* Pg. 65.

121   Bhandari, S.S., Koirala, P., Regmi, N., Pant, S. (2017). High Altitude Medical Biology, *Retinal Hemorrhage in a High-Altitude Aid Post Volunteer Doctor.* Vol. 18(3): 285-287. Abstract.

122   Ibid. Abstract.

123   Bjhende, M.P., Karpe, A.P., Pal, B.P. (November 23, 2019). Indian Journal of Ophthalmology, *High Altitude Retinopathy,* Abstract.

124   Lim, J.I., Stuart, K.V., Hartnett, M.E. (May 30, 2020). High altitude retinopathy. *American Academy of Opthamology.* Pg. 10.

125   U.S. Army – Altitude Acclimatization and Illness Management. *Op Cit.,* Pg. 65.

126   U.S. Army – Altitude Acclimatization and Illness Management, *Op Cit.,* Pgs. 66-67.

127   *Travel Health Guide.* Ibid. Pg. 73.

128   Altitude illness. *The Institute for Altitude Medicine.* P. 5.

129   Altitude illness. *The Institute for Altitude Medicine.* P. 6.

130   U.S. Army – Altitude Acclimatization and Illness Management, *Op Cit.,* Pg. 49.

131   Treating Sickness and Edema Caused by High Altitude. (2016). *Journal of Emergency Medical Services.* Pg. 6.

132   Luks, A.M, Swenson, E.R., Baertsch, P. (2017). Acute High-Altitude Sickness. *European Respiratory Review.* Pg. 6.

133   Netzer,, N., Strohl, K. Faulhaber, M. Gatterer, H. (July 1, 2013). Hypoxia-Related Altitude Illnesses, *Journal of Travel Medicine.* P. 251.

134   Journal of Emergency Medical Services *Op Cit.,* Pg.2.

135   Shortsleeve, C. (February 11, 2017). Can Oxygen Bars at Ski Resorts Really Help You Beat Altitude Sickness? *Conde Nast Traveler.* Pg. 1.

136   Shortsleeve, C. *Op Cit.* Pg. 2.

137   Altitude Illness – *The Institute for Altitude Medicine. Op Cit.* Pg. 1.

138 The Rise of Oxygen Bars, *WebMD*. Pg. 2.

139 Imray, C. (August 2011). Acute Altitude Illness. *Clinical Review.* Pg. 416.

140 Auerbach. Op Cit. Pg. 307.

141 Imray, C., *Op Cit.* Pg. 414.

142 Acetazolamide. (August 13, 2020). Altitude Sickness. Wikipedia. Pg. 2.

143 Afnan I. Al-Saleem and Asma M. Al-Jobair. (April 16, 2015). Possible association between acetazolamide administration during pregnancy and multiple congenital malformations. *Dove Press – Drug Design, Development and Therapy – Possible association between acetazolamide administration during pregnancy and multiple congenital malformations 10: Pgs. 1471-1476.*

144 Murdoch, D. (2010). Altitude Sickness. *British Journal of Medicine BJM.* Volume. P. 1218.

145 Altitude Sickness. (August 21, 2019). *Cigna* Pg. 2.

146 U.S. Army – Altitude Acclimatization and Illness Management. Op Cit. Pg.24.

147 Imray, C. Op Cit. Pg.343.

148 U.S. Army – Altitude Acclimatization and Illness Management. *Op Cit.* Pg. 17.

149 Auerbach. *Op Cit.* 307

150 U.S. Army – Altitude Acclimatization and Illness Management. *Op Cit.* Pg. 17.

151 Auerbach. *Op Cit.* Pg. 307.

152 U.S. Army – Altitude Acclimatization and Illness Management. *Op Cit.* Pg. 27.

153 European Respiratory Review. *Op Cit.* Pg. 15.

154 U.S. Army – Altitude Acclimatization and Illness Management. *Op Cit,* Pg. 15.

155 U.S. Army – Altitude Acclimatization and Illness Management. *Op Cit.* Pg. 53.

156 Luks. *Op Cit.* Pg. 15.

157 Altitude Illness – *The Institute for Altitude Medicine. Op Cit.* Pg. 5.

158 Imray, C., *Op Cit.* Pg. 415.

159 Tsai, T-Y., Wang, S-H., Lee, Y-K., Su, Y-C. (2018). Ginkgo biloba extract for prevention of acute mountain sickness: a systematic review and meta-analysis of randomized controlled trials. *British Medical Journal (BMJ).* Volume 8(8), Abstract.

160 Altitude Illness. *Institute for Alpine Medicine. Op Cit.* Pg. 2.

161 Netzger, N., *Op Cit.* Pg.4.

162 Vinnikov, D. Blanc P.D., Steinmaus, C. (June 2016). Is Smoking a Predictor for Acute Mountain Sickness? Findings From a Meta-Anaysis. *Nicotine and Tobacco Research*, Vol. 18, Issue 6. Pg. 167.

163 Tian-Yi Wu, et alia. (2011). Smoking, acute mountain sickness and altitude acclimatization: a cohort study. *BMJ Journals - Thorax.* Vol. 67, Issue 10. Pg. 2.

164 U.S. Army – Altitude Acclimatization and Illness Management. Op cit. Pg. 24.

165 Pre-existing Medical Conditions at Altitude. (2016-18). *Institute for Altitude Medicine at Telluride.* Mieske, K., Flaherty, G., O'Brien, T. (November 1, 2009). Journeys to High Altitude – Risks and Recommendations for Travelers with Preexisting Medical Conditions. *Journal of Travel Medicine.* Vol. 17, Issue 1 Pgs. 48-62.

166 Martin, R.S., Brito, J., Siques, P., Leon-Velarde, F. (August 16, 2017). Obesity Facts - Obesity as a Conditioning Factor for High-Altitude Diseases. *The European Journal of Obesity.* Pgs. 3, 7.

167 Pre-existing Medical Conditions at Altitude – How Does High Altitude Affect Pregnancy? *Op Cit.* Pg. 6.

168 *Ibid.* Pg. 5.

169 European Respiratory Review. *Op Cit.* Pg. 5.

170 Moore, L.G. (October 1999). Women at Altitude: Effects of Menstrual Cycle Phase and Alpha-Adrenergic Blockade on High Altitude Acclimatization. *University of Colorado Health Science Center.* Pg. 25.

171 Altitude illness. *The Institute for Altitude Medicine. Op Cit.* Pg. 6.

172   Stokes, S., Kalson, N.S., Earl, M., Whitehead, A.G., Tyrell-Marsh, I., Frost, H., Davies, A. (March 2010), Age is no barrier to success at very high altitudes. *Age and Aging,* Volume 39, Issue 2, Pg. 263.

173   U.S. Army – Altitude Acclimatization and Illness Management. Op cit. Pg. 18.

174   Fayed, N., P.J. Humberto Morales. (February 2006). Evidence of Brain Damage after High-altitude Climbing by Means of Magnetic Resonance Imaging. *The American Journal of Medicine,*
Volume 119, Issue 2. Abstract.

175   Gupton, N. (June 12, 2017). Ben Franklin and the Kite Experiment. *The Franklin Institute.*

176   Smyth, A.H. Ed. (1906). The Writings of Benjamin Franklin. *The Macmillan Company.* Vol. 5, Pgs. 42-422.

177   Lightning. (August 30, 2020). *Wikipedia – Distribution and Frequency.* Pgs. 4-5

178   Rank of Total Lightning Count Densities by State from 2015 to 2019. *Vaisala.* Pg. 2

179   Mistovich, J.J., et al. *Op Cit.* Pg. 2.

180   Lightning – General Considerations. (August 30, 2020). *Wikipedia.* Pg. 2-3.

181   Lightning. (August 30, 2020). *Wikipedia.* Pg. 1.

182   Hialele, B.M. (March 2016), Fulminology to Human Safety: A Case of N8 Road South Africa. *International Journal of Emergency Mental Health and Human Resilience.* Pg. 3.

183   Gookin. Lightning. *Op Cit.* Pg. 22.

184   Jensenius, J.S. Jr. Understanding Lightning Science. *National Weather Service.* Http//www. weather.gov/safety/lightning-science-review.

185   Jensenius, J.S. Jr. Understanding Lightning: Types of Flashes. *National Weather Service.* Http//www.weather.gov/safety/lightning-science-review.

186   National Weather Service – Lightning Myths and Facts. *Op Cit.* Pg. 2.

187   Jensenius, J.S. Jr. How Hot is Lightning? *National Weather Service.* weather.gov/safety/ lightning-science-review.

188   Lightning – Information for the Media. *National lightning Safety Institute.* Pg. 2.

189   Fulgurite. (August 24, 2020). *Wikipedia.*

190   Sweet Home Alabama. (September 3, 2020). *Wikipedia.* Pgs. 1-2.

191   Ibid. Pg. 2.

192   Lightning – Distribution and Frequency. *Op Cit.* Pg. 5.

193   Ball lightning: weird, mysterious, perplexing, and deadly. (March 5, 2019). *National Geographic.* Pg. 1.

194   St. Elmo's Fire. (September 2, 2020). *Wikipedia.*

195   What Causes the Smell After It Rains? (May 27, 2014). Gizmodo – Science. Pgs. 1-2.

196   Lightning. *Wikipedia. Op Cit.* Pg. 15.

197   Understanding Lightning: Thunder. *National Weather Service.*

198   Gookin, J. (2014). Lightning. *National Outdoor Leadership School.* Pg. 10.

199   Lightning. *Wikipedia. Op Cit.* Pg. 15.

200   Jensenius, J.S. Jr. Understanding Lightning Science. Pg. 2

201   Volcanic Lightning. *National Geographic – Resource Library.* Pg. 1.

202   National Weather Service – Lightning Myths and Facts. *Op Cit.* Pg. 1.

203   Information for the Media. *Op Cit.* Pg. 2.

204   Lightning - Physical Manifestations. (August 30, 2020). *Wikipedia.* Pg. 20.

205   Lightning Myths. *National Weather Service. Op Cit.* Pg. 2.

206   Bella Group. (June 12, 2012). Lightning Myths. *Lightning Protection Institute.* Pg. 2.

207   Jensenius, Jr., J. (February, 2020). A Detailed Analysis of Lightning Deaths in the United States from 2006 through 2019. *National Lightning Safety Council.* Pg. 5-6.

208 Rupke, E.J (August 14, 2006). What happens when lightning strikes an airplane? *Scientific American*. Pg. 5.

209 Faraday cage. (August 31, 2020) *Wikipedia*. Pg. 1.

210 Lightning Science: Five Ways Lightning Strikes People. *National Weather Service*. Pgs 1 – 3.

211 Gookin. Lightning. *Op Cit*. Pg. 36.

212 Gookin. Lightning. *Op Cit*. Pgs. 30-32.

213 Gookin. Lightning. *Op Cit*. Pg. 34.

214 Gookin. Lightning. *Op Cit*. Pg. 36

215 Gookin. Lightning. *Op Cit*. Pg. 12.

216 Gookin, Lightning. *Op Cit*. Pg. 35.

217 Watkins, G. (November 7, 2010). The hair raising truth about lightning. *Science and Tech*. Pg. 2.

218 Ehrlich, G. *Op Cit*. Pgs. 5-6.

219 Gookin. *Op Cit*. Pg. 43.

220 Lightning Injury. *Op Cit*. *Wikipedia*. Pg. 4.

221 Mistovich, *Op Cit*. Pg. 3.

222 National Geographic, *Op Cit*. Pg. 2.

223 Gookin. *Op Cit*. Pg. 45.

224 Lightning Injury. *Op Cit*. *Wikipedia*. Pg. 4.

225 Ehrlich, G. (1994). A Match to the Heart. *Penguin Books*. Pg.158.

226 Lightning Injury. (April 19, 2020). *Wikipedia*. P. 2.

227 Mistovich, *Op Cit*. Pg. 5.

228 Ehrlich, G. *Op Cit*. Pgs. 24-25.

229 Andrews, C.J., Reisner, A.D., Cooper, M.A. (September 2017). Post electrical or lightning injury syndrome. *Neural Regeneration Research*. P. 1406.

230 Flash Facts About Lightning. (2005). *National Geographic*. Pg. 1.

231 Gookin. *Op Cit*. Pg. 52.

232 Gookin. *Op Cit*. Pgs. 51-52.

233 Gookin. *Op Cit*. Pgs.42.

234 Faraday Cages. *Op Cit*. Pg. 4

235 Mikkelson, B. (June 27, 2009). Lightning Telephone Deaths. *Scopes*. NOAA Knows – Lightning. *National Oceanic and Atmospheric Administration*.

236 NOAAKnows – Lightning. *National Oceanic and Atmospheric Administration*.

237 Gookin. *Op Cit*. Pg. 31.

238 www.lightning-strike.org.

239 Baine, C. (April 20, 2013). Colorado's Loveland Pass Avalanche: Lessons Learned. *Outside Online*. Pgs. 1-2.

240 McGhee, T., (Dettman, P., Garcia, A. (April 21, 2013). Loveland avalanche victims identified from Colorado's deadliest slide in 50 years. *The Denver Post*. Pg. 2.

241 Lazar, B. (April 24, 2013). Colorado – Sheep Creel. North of Loveland Pass. *Colorado Avalanche Information Center*. Pgs. 1-7. This site also contains a brief video showing the aftermath of the Loveland Pass avalanche.

242 Baine. *Op Cit*. Pg. 6.

243 1999 Galteur Avalanche. (June 22, 2020). *Wikipedia*. Pgs. 1 – 3.

244 Nath. C. (June 3, 2013). Five men killed in Loveland Pass avalanche identified. *Summit Daily*. Pg. 1.

245 Fraser, S. (February 5, 2020). Avalanche in Turkey Wipes Out Rescue Team; 38 Dead Overall. *Associated Press*.

246 List of avalanches by death toll. (August 28, 2020). *Wikipedia*. Pg. 2.

247 1970 Ancash earthquake. (October 1, 2020). *Wikipedia*. Pg. 1.

248 Birkeland, K.W. Avalanche. *U.S. Forest Service National Avalanche Center.* Pg. 3.
249 LaChapelle, E.R. (July 11, 2002). Snow Avalanche. *Wasatch National Forest, Utah, U.S. Department of Agriculture. Pg. 4.*
250 All About Snow. (January 10, 2020). *National Snow and Ice Center.* Pg. 2.
251 Birkeland, K.W. *Op Cit.* Pg. 2.
252 Snow Avalanche- All About Snow. (January 10, 2020). *National Snow and Ice Data Center. Pg. 3.*
253 Elements of a Slide. *Nova Online. PBS*.orb/wgbh/nova/avalanche/elements. Pg. 1.
254 LaChapelle, Ibid. Pg.
255 Snow layers. Ibid.
256 Avalanche. (September 23, 2020). *Wikipedia.* Pg. 3.
257 Avalanche. Ibid. P.9.
258 Avalanche. *Avalanche.org/avalanche-encyclopedia/avalanche. Op Cit.* Pg. 1.
259 Avalanche – Wikipedia. *Op Cit.* Pg.4.
260 Avalanche. *Avalanche.org/avalanche-encyclopedia/avalanche. Op Cit.* Pgs. 4-5.
261 Avalanche. *Avalanche.org/avalanche-encyclopedia/avalanche. Op Cit.* Pgs. 3-7.
262 2014 Mount Everest ice avalanche. (July 27, 2020). *Wikipedia.* Pg. 1.
263 2015 Mount Everest avalanches. (October 14, 2020). *Wikipedia.* Pg. 1.
264 Cornice. Avalanche.org/avalanche-encyclopedia/cornice. *American Avalanche Association.*
265 LaChapelle, E.R. *Op Cit.* Pg.3.
266 LaChapelle, E.H. *Op Cit.* Pg. 6.
267 Safe Riders Snowmobile Safety Awareness Program – Section 5, Overview. *Saferiderssafetyawarenessorg/avoiding-avalanches-while-snowmobiling.html.*
268 Kirkland, K.W. Opacity. Pg. 4.
269 Reuter, B. and Schweitzer, Jeer. (2009). Avalanche triggering by sound: myth and truth. *Institute for Snow and Avalanche Research.* Pg. 1.
270 LaChapelle, E.R. *Op Cit.* Pg. 7.
271 Maggart, L. (October 16, 2017). How does it work? Starting an avalanche: CDOT preps Gazex avalanche exploders for coming winter months. *Sky-Hi News.* Pg. 2.
272 Avalanche. *Wikipedia. Op Cit.* Pg. 11
273 1999 Galteur Avalanche. *Op Cit.* Pg. 3.
274 Birkeland, K.W. *Op Cit.* Pg. 3.
275 Anchors – Avalanche Encyclopedia. *Avalanche.org-avalanche-encyclopedia/#anchors.* Pg. 3.
276 Camarino, A. (August 28, 2020). Using Reforestation for Avalanche Mitigation: Does it Work? *Snowbrains.com/using-reforestation-for-avalanche-mitigation-does-it-work/*
277 LaChapelle, E.R. *Op Cit.* Pg. 7.
278 Wyssen Avalanche Control. (2020). https://www.wyssenavalanche.com/en/avalanche-detection/
279 Shoud You Use An Avalung? (February 7, 2018). *Powder Magazine.*
280 How To Use Avalanche Safety Gear. *REI Coop. rei.com/learn/expert-advice/avalanche-safety-gear.html*
281 Sommers, J. (March 23, 2020). Snow Science Against the Avalanche. *Annals of Nature.* P. 4.
282 Inglis-Arkell. (February 26, 2015). Why Freezing to Death Makes You Want to Get Naked. *Gizmodo.* Pgs. 1-2.
283 Hypothermia. (October 19, 2020). *Wikipedia.* Pg. 1.
284 Zafren, K., Mechem, C.C. (May 13, 2020). Accidental hypothermia in adults. *Uptodate.* Pg. 1.
285 Zafren, K., Mechem, C.C. *Op Cit.* Pg.10.
286 Guly, H. (July 29, 2010). History of accidental hypothermia. *Resuscitation.* Pg. 3.
287 Kaplan, R. (2000). Medicine at the Battle of Stalingrad. *Journal of the Royal Society of Medicine – 93:97-98.* Pgs. 97-98.

288   Hasselbach, C. (February 2, 2018). Russia marks Stalingrad defeat of Nazis.

289   Hypothermia. *Wikipedia. Op Cit.* Pg.8.

290   Martin, J.D. *Op Cit.* Pg.1.

291   Mikeachim. (July 15,2020). This is Your Body As It Freezes. *Fevered Mutterings.* Pg. 1

292   McCullough, L. and Aroka, S. (December 2004). Diagnosis and Treatment of Hypothermia. *American Family Physician.* Pgs. 3-4.

293   Hypothermia. *Wikipedia. Op Cit.* Pgs. 3-4.

294   What is cold diuresis? (February 13, 2017). Arkansas Urology. Pgs.1 – 2.

295   Hypothermia. *Wikipedia. Op Cit.* Pg. 4.

296   Hypothermia: What It Is, What to Do. (January 19, 2017). *University of California, Berkeley – Wellness.* Pg. 2.

297   Stark, P. (January 1999). Frozen Alive. *Outside Online.* P. 9.

298   Zafren, K. and Mechem, C.C. *Op Cit.* Pg. 1.

299   Zafren, K., and Mechem, C.C. Ibid. Pg. 1.

300   Hypothermia. *Wikipedia. Op Cit.* Pg 4.

301   Stark, P. *Op Cit.* Pg. 5.

302   Hypothermia. *Wikipedia. Op Cit.* Pg. 4.

303   Inglis-Arkell, E. *Op Cit.* Pg. 2.

304   Hypothermia. *Wikipedia. Op Cit.* Pg.5.

305   McCullough and Arora. OpCit. Pg. 3.

306   Ainslie, P.N., Reilly, T. (2003). Physiology of accidental hypothermia in the mountains: a forgotten story. *British Journal of Sports Medicine.* P. 4

307   Ainslie, P.N., Reilly, T. *Op Cit.* P. 4.

308   Castellani, J.W. *Op Cit.* Pg. 1.

309   Young, A.J. and Castellani, J.W. (June 18, 2007). Exceptional Fatigue and Cold Exposure: Mechanisms of Hikers Hypothermia. *Canadian Science Publishing.* Abstract.

310   Ainslie, P.N., Reilly, T. *Op Cit.* Pg. 3.

311   Ainslie, P.N., Reilly, T. *Op Cit.* Pg. 6.

312   McCullough and Anorka *Op Cit.* Pg. 4.

313   Dharmarajan, T.X. and Widjiaja. (December 12, 2007). Hypothermia in the geriatric population. *Future Medicine. Pg. 1, abstract.*

314   Mayo Clinic Staff. (April 18, 2020). Hypothermia. *Mayo Clinic.* Pg. 3.

315   Guly, H. *Op Cit.* Pg. 6.

316   Morrissey, S. (February 5, 2015). Two things to remember about winter exploring. *Lake Placid.* P. 1-2.

317   Zafren, K. and Mechem, C.C *Op Cit.* Pg. 7.

318   Hypothermia. *Wikipedia. Op Cit.* Pg. 5.

319   Castellani, J.W. *Op Cit.* Pg. 3.

320   Zafren, K., Mechem, C.C. *Op Cit.* Pg. 3.

321   Do We Really Lose Most of Our Heat Through Our Heads? *WebMS.* Pg. 2

322   Sample, I. (December 17, 2008). Scientists debunk the myth that you lose most heat through your head. *The Guardian.* Pg. 2.

323   Mayo Clinic Staff. *Op Cit.* Pg. 3.

324   Stark, P. Pg. 2.

325   Hunting Reaction. (November 20, 2019). *Wikipedia.* Pg. 1.

326   Park, W. (February 27, 2020). The man who refused to refused to freeze to death. *BBC Future.* Pg. 3.

327   Park, W. *Op Cit.* Pg. 7.

328   McCullough, L. and Aroka, S. (December 2004). Diagnosis and Treatment of Hypothermia. *American Family Physician.* Pg. 9.

329   Zafrem, K. and Mechem, C.C. *Op Cit.* Pg. 9.

330   Afterdrop. *Wikipedia. Op Cit.* Pg. 1.

331   Zafrem, K. and Mechem, C.C. *Op Cit.* Pg. 10.

332   Dietrichs, E.F., Haeheim, B., Kondratiev, T. Traasdahl, E., Tveita, T. (April 12, 2018). Effects of hypothermia and rewarming on cardiovascular autonomic control in vivo. *Applied Physiology.* Pg. 2, abstract.

333   Stark, P. *Op Cit.* Pg. 7.

334   McCullough, L. and Aroka, S. *Op Cit.* Pg. 10.

335   Hypothermia: What It Is, What to Do. (January 19, 2017). *University of California – Berkeley Wellness.* Pg.2.

336   Hypothermia. *Wikipedia. Op Cit.* Pg. 9.

337   Hypothermia. Wikipedia. *Op Cit.* Pg.9.

338   Cold Shock Response. Wikipedia. *Op Cit.* Pg. 25.

339   The Mammalian Diving Response. (March 11, 2012). *Dartmouth Undergraduate Journal of Science.* Pg. 3.

340   Girl survives 13-degree body temperature. (September 22, 2014). *MSN Wellbeing.* Pgs. 2-3.

341   McCullough, L. *Op Cit.* Pg. 3.

342   Hypothermia. Wikipedia. *Op Cit.* Pg.9.

343   Hypothermia. Wikipedia. *Op Cit.* Pg. 8.

344   Brunette, D. (January 2018). Cold truths about hypothermia. *Hennepin Health Care News.* Pg.2.

345   Rosenthal, M. (January 3, 2020). Maternal hypothermia from environmental exposure in the third trimester. *International Journal of Circumpolar Health* Pg. 2.

346   Davies, M. (September 1, 2016). How a heatwave can harm your baby: Being too hot or during pregnancy
May increase the risk of premature birth. *MailOnline.* Pg. 1.

347   Acclimatization (adjusting to the temperature). (October 2016). *University of Iowa Hospitals and Clinics.* Pg. 1.

348   Berger, R.L. (May 17, 1990). Nazi Science – The Dachau Hypothermia Experiments. *New England Journal of Medicine.* P. 1435.

349   Hypothermia. Wikipedia. *Op Cit.* Pg.11.

350   Hypothermia in Dogs: Symptoms and Treatment. *Purina.* Pgs. 1-4.

CPSIA information can be obtained
at www.ICGtesting.com
Printed in the USA
LVHW102012110821
694978LV00010B/72